WORK at HOME

In Caitlin's new book, she dishes the dirt on working from home—her no-secrets, no-holds-barred approach is relatable *and* doable. I also love that this book applies to someone already working from home as well as someone aspiring to work from home. She lists legitimate business ideas for someone looking to work from home, and she includes a 28-day launch plan at the end—perfect for putting what you learn into practice!

Becky Rapinchuk
CleanMama.net

I've known Caitlin for a couple of years now, and I'm blown away by her success. She's taught thousands of people how to make money from home—she knows her stuff! If you want to skip the guesswork and learn what it really takes to be successful working at home, then you can trust Caitlin to teach you how.

Michelle Schroeder-Gardner
MakingSenseOfCents.com

If you're looking for an easy-to-digest guide to working from home, this is it. This book will inspire and motivate you while giving you practical and easy-to-understand steps to make your dream a reality. Bonus points because it's written by a woman who has actually done it—in several different jobs!

Rosemarie Groner
BusyBudgeter.com

You can trust Caitlin to tell it like it is. She tirelessly shares fluff-free advice perfect for beginners. Cutting through the BS, Caitlin gives you clear steps to get out of your own way and do what it takes to create the life you've always wanted.

Steve Olsher
SteveOlsher.com

From the moment I met Caitlin, I could tell she was going to make waves in the work-at-home industry. In a niche full of programs promising shortcuts and easy paydays, Caitlin's content, courses, and presence online are filled with hopeful but realistic, actionable steps to make a full-time income from home.

She's an influencer who encourages small beginnings, celebrates the daily wins, and doesn't shrink back when the hard questions come as to why some people become wildly successful and others don't. *Work At Home* is unique because she tackles many of the real obstacles in an aspiring entrepreneur's path. Many obstacles have nothing to do with some get-rich-quick scheme or secret. They are our choices, our mindset, our commitment to the process of learning a skill that can be leveraged and is valuable in the online marketplace. For anyone getting started with the work-at-home journey: Caitlin has paved the way for others who are looking for real help, growth, and success.

Julie Stoian
JulieStoian.com

If you're looking for a solid, step-by-step guide to achieving the flexibility and freedom that working from home—or from anywhere!—allows, then you've definitely picked up the right book. Caitlin's straightforward, non-sugarcoated, action-oriented guidance will lead you through the process of exploring your options, identifying your skills, narrowing down the best potential fits (while identifying scams), and then launching your new endeavor. She busts open the limiting beliefs and myths so many of us hold around money, education, work, and success. She empowers readers to understand the power of investing in yourself and taking decisive action. *Work At Home* is a must-read for anyone who is interested in harnessing their unlimited potential and leveraging it into a self-directed, rewarding, and lucrative career.

Mark Timm
CEO of Ziglar Family

Are you ready? You are holding in your hands the secret manual guaranteed to shortcut you to your dream life. Caitlin's superpower is to help people defy the odds, destroy self-doubt, and deploy almost *instantly* into a successful career working at home. I can't tell you how she does it. All I can tell you is *do what Caitlin says.*

Eileen Wilder, bestselling author & speaker
EileenWilder.com

Not only is Caitlin a good friend, she's the kind of friend who wants to help in everything she does. I highly recommend reading *and* implementing this no-bull guide to finding your pathway to not only work from home, but work from home *and* produce income!

Rachael Todd
RachaelTodd.com

Caitlin Pyle is a woman on a mission. That mission is helping others achieve a lifestyle they can only imagine through working from home (or anywhere, really!). We're in the midst of a revolution to take back control of our lives, starting with making our work **work for us,** and Caitlin's leading the charge!

Gina Horkey
HorkeyHandbook.com

Caitlin is a powerhouse—creative, energetic, and highly innovative. She's the expert in understanding the new normal of working from home (or anywhere) and is the pro to listen to on the subject. She takes no prisoners, so look out—she'll make you successful, fast.

Susie Moore
Susie-Moore.com

WORK*at* HOME

The NO-NONSENSE GUIDE to Avoiding Scams and Generating Real Income from ANYWHERE!

CAITLIN PYLE

NEW YORK

LONDON • NASHVILLE • MELBOURNE • VANCOUVER

Work At Home
The NO-NONSENSE GUIDE to Avoiding Scams and Generating Real Income from ANYWHERE!

© 2019 Caitlin Pyle

Published in New York, New York, by Morgan James Publishing.
Morgan James is a trademark of Morgan James, LLC.
www.MorganJamesPublishing.com

The Morgan James Speakers Group can bring authors to your live event. For more information or to book an event visit The Morgan James Speakers Group at www.TheMorganJamesSpeakersGroup.com.

ISBN 978-1-64279-168-6 paperback
ISBN 978-1-64279-169-3 eBook
Library of Congress Control Number: 2018950128

Cover Design by:
Chris Kirk
Author Photo by:
Ben Perry
BenPerry.co

Interior Design by:
Megan Whitney Dillon
Creative Ninja Designs
megan@creativeninjadesigns.com

In an effort to support local communities, raise awareness and funds, Morgan James Publishing donates a percentage of all book sales for the life of each book to Habitat for Humanity Peninsula and Greater Williamsburg.

Get involved today! Visit
www.MorganJamesBuilds.com

This book is dedicated to you. Yes; you—the person reading this right now! You have an infinite capacity for serving others with your unique skills, and I'm so excited to be on this journey with you. Keep doing the hard things; keep learning and serving while others are waiting and wishing… and watch your life—and the world!—transform.

CONTENTS

Foreword   xiii

Preface   xxi

Introduction   xxiii

Warning   xxxi

How to Use This Book   xxxv

Part 1: Behind the Curtain—From Supermarket to Success   1

     Chapter 1: Will Work for Pay:

           My First Attempts at Making Money   3

     Chapter 2: The Awakening   9

     Chapter 3: Fired to Freelancing   19

     Chapter 4: Freelancing into Freedom   25

Part 2: 3 Steps to Work-From-Anywhere Freedom   33

Step 1: Free Your Mind from the Lies that Hold You Back   33

     Chapter 5: Why These Lies Hold You Back   35

     Chapter 6: The Truth About Money   41

     Chapter 7: The Truth About Education   51

     Chapter 8: The Truth About Work   61

     Chapter 9: The Truth About Business and Success   73

Step 2: Level Up Your Mind and Your Skills   89

     Investing in Yourself

     Chapter 10: Why What Worked for Someone Else

            Won't Necessarily Work for You   93

     Chapter 11: Investing in Yourself and Your Future   103

Chapter 12: Real Wealth
(and the Scarcest Resource on Earth)   115

The Scams and You
Chapter 13: Getting Real about Scams   123
Chapter 14: Spotting and Avoiding Scams   127
Chapter 15: How *You* Can Avoid Becoming a Scam   135

Identifying Your Best Options
Chapter 16: The Fastest Way to Start   141
Chapter 17: Finding Your Best Long-Term Fit   147
Chapter 18: Your List of Legitimate Work-At-Home Ideas 153
Chapter 19: Identifying Your Top 5 Best Options to Consider 165
Chapter 20: Filtering Your Top 5 Ideas   171
Chapter 21: Setting Yourself Up for Your 28-Day Launch 181

Step 3: Launch   187
Chapter 22: Your 28-Day Launch Plan   189

Final Words of Wisdom   215
Acknowledgments   221
About the Author   225

FOREWORD
Katie Chase, MomIsMore.com

My story is like many others' stories. In fact, there's nothing particularly special about my story at all. I'm a mom, a wife, a dog owner, a homeowner, a sister, a daughter, etc. And like many, I rely on faith to get me through every day.

We all have stories and struggles. Each of us wakes up every single day facing challenges no one else knows anything about. Struggles of the mind, struggles of the heart, struggles of the body, struggles of the wallet...

You get the idea.

But what makes one story rise up above another? What makes someone stop and say, "Hey, that story is a little bit different"?

To answer that, I want to share with you the story of my journey that has led me to this moment—*writing the foreword for this powerful book.*

This part of my story starts in 2010. My husband and I had just finished a two-and-a-half-year stint taking care of his grandmother in California until she passed away. It was one of the most challenging seasons of my life—*a new bride in a new family intimately caring for a woman I hardly knew.*

There were *many* days I felt that I didn't belong, nor did I have what it took to see it through for the long haul. Many days were fraught with depression and frustration. There were also days that helped me solidify my purpose in that tumultuous time—*Grandma Marge needed someone's compassion and care. End of discussion.*

Our time with Grandma passed slowly, but still, it passed. In the end, it was a bittersweet parting. It left me with a deeper understanding of what it took to face things that feel so much bigger than me.

We left California to start our new adventure. Donnie and I found ourselves at home in the Pacific Northwest—Portland, Oregon. Donnie transferred his job at Michaels Arts and Crafts up to Portland, and we followed the open door.

Shortly thereafter, we found ourselves facing a very unexpected surprise—*we were pregnant.* It was a rocky pregnancy at the start, discovered after a trip to the emergency room, which landed me on antibiotic suppression for the duration of my pregnancy. Still, all was well enough for me to go back to work in the classroom as an assistant teacher. In my last trimester, I experienced preterm labor. I was forced to hang up my teaching apron and start my two months of bed rest until our son or daughter made his or her debut.

Labor and delivery came, as did another trial-by-fire, life-altering experience—a grueling 21-hour labor, which culminated in an emergency C-section that had a potentially fatal complication. What was supposed to be a gentle ushering into motherhood turned out to be a formidable smackdown I never saw coming.

I wasn't prepared. And I had no friggin' clue what I was doing. I had to remind myself every single day that I was a survivor, and I was going to figure. it. out.

Three years into motherhood, life once again threw us a curveball, as it's so known for doing. Our son, the catalyst for the smackdown of motherhood, had special needs.

Special. Needs.

Once again, life required adaptation on our part, and so we complied. We attended appointments, therapy sessions, meetings, etc. We loved, hugged, kissed, and read a zillion stories. We watched movies, we laughed, and we cried... *a lot.*

And all of a sudden, I found myself clambering for any kind of perseverance—*any kind of courage I could muster*—so I could get through from day to day.

Amidst all of the life happenings surrounding our precious, firecracker son, we added another sweet baby to our family. During that time, my husband found himself working 12–16 hours a day at a job where he was very underappreciated and neglected.

He would wake up before the sun, leave us warm in our beds, and come back just in time for dinner and bedtime. On work days, we saw him for maybe an hour. My days became lonelier, spent at home juggling my oldest son's needs with the daily to-dos of parenting an infant, keeping the house clean*ish,* and surviving the day-to-day experiences.

It was an isolating time. We had no family nearby. Because of our son's special dietary and behavioral needs, we were rarely able to spend time with friends—*or even make them to begin with.*

This was our life. This was the struggle we faced. It wasn't a unique struggle. It wasn't even an uncommon struggle in today's world. But it was ours—*our very own struggle for daily perseverance and courage.* Sometimes we found it. Sometimes we just kept looking. But we resolved to always look for it, no matter what the day would bring us.

One night after Donnie got home and the kids were tucked into bed, I poured out my heart right there on the half-cleared, crumb-encrusted dinner table. It was time. Something needed to give.

After seven and a half years of taking care of other humans, I suddenly found myself empty and, honestly, *lost.* I felt like there was so much inside of me that had been buried deep inside during those years of pouring out myself for others. My identity had been wrapped up in my title.

Mom. Caregiver. Wife.

But who was Katie? What made her tick? What was it that made her who she was?

In my pursuit of rediscovering who I was (but not really knowing what I was looking for), we decided that night at the dinner table that it was time that I started investing a little in myself.

I ~~wanted~~ *needed* to invest in myself in a way that proved to be a benefit to our family. And with the new healthcare law taking effect, I knew I needed to bring in money to help supplement our family's income and offset healthcare costs.

So I decided to focus some of that inward tension and turmoil to solve an outward problem. *I was going to start training to learn a new skill so we could earn more money.*

The solution? I was going to start going to school—*well, sort of*. I was going to learn a skill—something that could sustain us if anything (God forbid!) ever happened to Donnie, who was at the time the sole breadwinner of the family.

I had no idea where this choice would take me. I had hustled my way into side income after side income over the last four and a half years. I did anything from repairing used children's shoes to sell at consignment, to fixing up used children's clothes for resale, to painting and refurbishing furniture. But none of these things provided any kind of steady income.

I had two uncompromisable criteria that I required in any sort of investment I made in myself: 1) I had to be able to do it from home, and 2) I had to be able to go at my own pace. Life often demands us to comply, and this time wasn't any different.

And so I started a new adventure in a search for something to help me achieve my goal: *skills*.

I had recently seen a unique course that would teach me how to proofread for court reporters. I was highly skeptical (*to say the least*). Like most folks looking for a legit side hustle, I've seen *all* the scams out there. I wasn't about to be taken for a ride. But it was time for me to dip into that courage and take that first step—*because what if it isn't a scam? What if it's the first step to a lifetime of change?*

I *had* to find out.

Truth be told, I was terrified. What if this turned out to be another failed attempt at making money? What if it turned out to be a huge scam and I lost all of my tuition money to it? What would I tell Donnie if I wasted our family's money on something that wasn't real?

So right there at that dinner table, Donnie, being unwaveringly supportive as he always was, said, "Do it. Even if it proves to be a scam, you have to try if for no other reason than to say you did it."

Case closed. I enrolled that night.

I vetted the course with an endless number of emails to the course creator, Caitlin Pyle. I plowed ahead through this new-to-me training program to learn a skill I never even knew existed. I became a proofreader for court reporters, *and in the process, discovered an insatiable love of learning.*

I juggled studying during nap times, after bedtime, and during my husband's days off until finally I graduated the course. After working successfully as a trained proofreader, I decided I wanted more. So I decided to take a transcription course, too.

And I could hardly believe that I was starting to earn a solid part-time income—*more* than enough to cover our healthcare costs.

But even more than that, I was slowly discovering pieces of myself that I hadn't seen in many, *many* years. It was like this whole other part of me had woken up that I didn't even know existed. And for the first time in what felt like forever, I started realizing that I could do far more than I ever thought I could.

I had a new trajectory in life—and I couldn't wait to see where it was going to take me.

It wasn't long after working as a transcriptionist that I discovered a deep love for virtual assisting. It blew open huge possibilities as I discovered highly sought-after skill sets that were waiting to be learned—*like low-hanging fruit waiting to be picked!*

So I rolled my proofreading and transcription skills into virtual assisting. I was hungry for skills and found so much joy in helping Caitlin, who was my first VA client, grow and maintain her business, while learning one more skill after another.

And within a year, I found myself working as a full-time work-at-home project manager for a big-name blogger.

So how long did it take me to go from new student to full-time working project manager? A year and a half. And in that time, my husband was able to quit his job to stay home with our boys. We were able to leave the revolving door of apartment hopping to purchase our own home. We were even able to purchase a service dog for our oldest son!

Our lives changed forever with the conversation we had at the dinner table that night. Looking back, I couldn't imagine what our lives would look like now had I not taken that first scary step toward the unknown.

So what makes a common, everyday story into an extraordinary one? **Two bootstraps called *perseverance* and *courage.***

They transformed Caitlin Pyle from fired proofreader into a multimillion-dollar work-at-home leader—*and the author of this book.*

They transformed me from a lost, burnt-out mom into a new woman with a full-time work-at-home career that I LOVE... into a mom who has more margin for her family... into a person who knows exactly who she is and what she's capable of.

And they can transform you, too.

Perseverance and courage, friend. That's all you need to change... well, everything.

So here's my question to you: When will your journey start?

Answer?

It already has.

Katie Chase
MomIsMore.com

PREFACE

The two biggest things I want you to get out of reading this book are 1) a clear understanding of what is required of you if you want to earn money—you must solve problems!—and 2) how much control *you* have over your own income.

With the mind-blowing power of the internet, it doesn't matter where you live, what your spouse does for a living, how many kids you have, what year you graduated from college, or even if you never went to college at all.

What does matter? What's between your ears and how you use it. The human brain is more capable than many of us believe, and making the conscious decision to own and harness its power—harness *your* power—will transform your life.

So with that, I want to introduce you to the Work-At-Home Hero Manifesto. It's a simple reminder of what making money is all about—and who's in charge of earning it: *you.*

I believe I am made for more.

I deserve to succeed financially.

My past doesn't dictate my future.

If I can solve problems, I can make money.

I write my own income story...

...and I am the Hero.

To your success,

Caitlin

P.S. — You can snag a printable 8.5" x 11" poster of the manifesto plus a sweet wallpaper graphic for your phone on the Resources page at WorkAtHomeSchool.com/BookResources

INTRODUCTION

What if you could make an *extra* $500, $1,000, or even $10,000 per month by doing something you're great at and enjoy doing? What if you never had to please an *impossible-to-please* boss ever again? What if you could **work wherever you want, whenever you want,** and ***wearing* whatever you want**... even your favorite sweatpants? Wouldn't it be fabulous to be able to do all the things your day job makes impossible and instead get to...

- Decide what days your "weekend" will be. Make commuter traffic and crazy weekend crowds a thing of the past.

- Schedule doctors' appointments right away. Take all the open appointments the nine-to-fivers have to pass up! Work whenever you want (and wherever you want... even the doctor's waiting room).

- Take a *romantic getaway* in the middle of the week. Have the entire bed & breakfast to yourselves. Even better, pay a fraction of the price the nine-to-fivers pay to get packed in like sardines on the weekends.

- Make enough money to **finally pay off your debt**—*like in full*. Get out from under the mound of student loan, credit card, or car debt you've been fighting for years...

Each one of those things is possible. I know because it's the reality for me and thousands of others. There's no reason it can't be the reality for you, too. All you need to do is unlock the hidden world of work-from-anywhere income. The best part is that you already have the key to that world—it's *you.*

We all hold the key. Yet millions of people still drag themselves out of bed every morning. After rushing to get ready, they sit in unbearable traffic or stuffed into an overcrowded bus or train. They spend all day working a job they hate for an unreasonable boss. They're paid just enough to make it to the next paycheck.

I know. That used to be me.

I used to *hate* my job. I used to hate my puny paycheck. I couldn't stand my office. It was soul-crushing. They even made me feel like I owed them *big time* for taking time off for my own honeymoon. I hated pretty much everything about it and desperately wanted to quit. But like many people, I couldn't pull the trigger. I did the same miserable things with the same miserable people every day until August 2011... when I got fired! I didn't *just* get fired, though. I got fired like you see in the movies... one of my bosses called me a "worthless pig" on my way out the door and accused me of stealing from the company. Another even told me I shouldn't have children and that I would "die alone."

More details on that later. The important part is that was the *last time* I ever worked for anyone else.

After getting fired, I started working as a freelance proofreader. I grew that business to a full-time income, then into a full-blown company with more than 20 team members—all in the span of six years. As my business grew, the team and I helped more and more people break free from the crippling self-doubt that plagued them. We did that by equipping them with powerful skills they could use to generate their own income from anywhere. Way too many people think they can't opt out of the day-job workforce like I did. The truth is, anyone can make a better life for themselves and their families if they want to. *It's a choice.*

Using the power of the internet, we've since trained thousands of people to turn real skills into real money. Many students have made extra money for groceries, cars, rent, and mortgages. Some even replaced or exceeded their day-job income—and some left their day jobs for good.

Will you be next? The choice is yours. I've broken the whole process down right here in this book, and there's even a 28-day action plan at the end. But take note: It's called an *action plan* for a reason. You must take action to achieve success. There are no exceptions; there's no magic wand that can make you the exception. You have to work for it. By the end of this book, I'm confident you'll *want* to work for it because you'll see what's possible for your life if you do.

3 Steps to Work-From-Anywhere Freedom

There are three steps that anyone reading this book can take to create work-from-anywhere freedom. Before I tell you the steps, I want to discuss the word *steps*. Notice I didn't say *theories*. It doesn't take three *theories* to succeed; it takes *steps*. You need to *take action* if you want to succeed. Taking these three *steps* can get you where you want to go.

Am I sounding like a broken record yet? I hope so. In the years I've spent training people to work at home, the concept of *taking action* is the most difficult for work-at-home newbies to grasp. The average person *does not* connect the dots between their [lack of] actions and their [lack of] success. I'd say, therefore, that the overlying goal for this book is to make sure you understand that concept. Do stuff? Stuff happens. Don't do stuff? *Nothing* happens. It's simple.

Okay; now that that's out in the open, I'd like to introduce you to the three steps.

Step 1: Free your mind from the lies that hold you back.

We've *all* heard—and learned to believe—all kinds of lies about education, money, work, business, and success. The truth is, you don't need college or student loans to make money. You can learn everything you need to know to make money working at home without going to college or into massive debt. You can actually make *more* money working at home than most people earn after spending four (or more!) years in college!

You also don't need to spend an hour every day stuck in traffic. You don't need to spend 40 or 50 hours a week working for a demanding boss to barely make enough money to feed your family. You don't need to hire a big team. You don't need a loan or an investor. And you *don't* need to work 100 hours a week to start a business that can transform your life.

Every work-at-home business is different. You can build one that fits exactly what *you* want for your life. I know hundreds of full-time work-at-home entrepreneurs, and many of them work less and earn more than when they worked a full-time job.

I'll show you exactly how my students and I freed our minds from the lies and changed the way we make money. Freeing your mind is non negotiable if you want to start earning part- or full-time income at home (or anywhere), so pay close attention!

Step 2: Level up your mind and your skills.

Once you free your mind of the lies that have held you back, it's time to level up your mind. Replace the garbage with gold. The best way to level up your mind is to *learn*. Picture yourself filling your mind with information and powerful skills you can use to create the life of your dreams. *That's* learning, and oftentimes you'll have to do that *before* you're comfortable… but once you do it, it can change everything. Got that? *Learning changes everything.* So what should you learn, exactly? Three things…

First, learn how to invest in yourself. You need to commit to investing in yourself and your future. This means not just choosing something because it worked for someone else, but finding something that's a good fit for *your* skills and interests. It means continuing to level up your skills so you can improve your impact and income—and using your resources wisely.

Second, learn to avoid the way-too-many scams that exist in the work-at-home world. I'll help you become one of the best scam spotters in the industry so you'll *never* get ripped off again. I'll also help you avoid accidentally *becoming* a scammer yourself. Yes; even *you* can become a scammer if you're not careful!

Third, learn the most promising opportunity for *you* and how to take action to pursue it. It has to be a legitimate opportunity that fits your skills, passions, and personality.

So many people stall out during these initial action steps because they lack confidence. Here's the thing about confidence: It flourishes right along with your skills. If you don't feel 100% confident in your skills, then don't expect to have the confidence you need to market those skills. On the other hand, if you do the work and commit to leveling up your skills—commit to *learning*—you'll ooze confidence! *Ooze.* I love that word. Oh, and if you're freaking out at the thought of marketing yourself right now, just remember that marketing is a skill you can learn just like everything else.

Don't worry; I've been there already, and I survived. I'm here to help you now! Next up, we've got one more step to cover. It piggybacks off the confidence theme...

Step 3: Launch.

The third step to work-from-anywhere freedom is to launch—to *start making money*. Sounds good, right? It can be scary, but it's not complicated… especially after freeing your mind and leveling up. Don't skip those steps! You might *think* you'll get there faster by skipping ahead, but you won't. Sometimes you have to slow down to speed up. Clearing the path ahead of time makes the journey far less rocky.

Look, you're *never* going to feel ready. Author and motivational speaker, Zig Ziglar, famously said "If you wait until all the lights are green before you leave home, you'll never get started on your trip to the top." It's so true. There are times when I'm launching a product or adding a team member that I *still* don't feel ready to "leave home." If you wait to feel ready, you'll *never* launch. Maybe you'll switch jobs; maybe your boss will leave, but your life will be pretty much the same next year as it is right now unless you *do something different* than you're doing now. You can either spin wheels, or you can take action.

Here's some inspiring news. There has been *no* better time than right now to start working at home. More and more companies have made a major shift away from the traditional 40-hour-per-week employment structure. They're hiring more freelancers. Why? It saves the companies time to recruit, vet, and interview people. It helps them avoid making long-term employment commitments. It also limits their financial outlay, which helps them afford higher-quality work from specialists. This *big* shift means *big* opportunities for people like you and me.

Take a deep breath. Don't freak out—there is plenty of opportunity for everyone, and it's only growing every day. At the end of this book, I'll walk you through exactly how to launch your own work-from-anywhere business with the 28-day launch plan.

This book contains **everything you need** to start your very own work-at-home business. Shut out any voice (internal or external) who's ever said you can't do it. Chances are, those voices belong to someone who *hasn't done it* and likely never will. I have done it; I am doing it; and I've taught thousands of others to do it, too. I'm here to tell you that you *can* skip your commute, enjoy your work, and unlock unlimited earning potential. You *can*.

In fact, the concepts you'll learn in this book helped me *double* my freelancing income within one year of business. Within seven years, my income grew from $2,000 per month to over $200,000 per month. That's not a typo—my income grew from $2,000 per month to $200,000 per month within the span of just seven years. Don't get me wrong; I'm *not* saying you'll generate more than $200,000 per month in seven years, but I *am* saying the exact same concepts you'll learn in this book got me there.

I'm not an anomaly. I don't have a genius-level IQ. I am a normal woman who struggles with the *same* stuff you might be struggling with right now (yes; even that). This book contains many harrowing, true details of the rocky path I took to get here. I'll never, ever tell you it was easy… but I'll always tell you it was worth it.

On that note, one warning before we get started…

WARNING

This book contains everything you need to begin building your own income from home. I'll teach you how to fill your mind with empowering beliefs and skills that will get you where you want to go. I'll share all my secrets for spotting scams. I'll even give you a 28-day launch plan to give you confidence, build momentum, and stay on track. I will push you to take action.

But there's one thing you *won't* get in this book. *Fluff.* I don't sugarcoat *anything*. Making money at home is simple. It *really* is. I've trained thousands of people all over the world to do it, and you know what? I've yet to meet anyone who *couldn't*. I've met plenty of people who *didn't*… but not a single person who *couldn't*.

There's really only *one thing* standing between you and making money from Hawaii, Lake Tahoe, Tahiti, or your sofa.

That one thing is *skills*.

Developing the Skills You Need to Build Work-From-Anywhere Income

Too many people skip over the *skill-building* part. They skip straight to selling with only mediocre skills and don't work to improve those skills. Some people don't think they should have to learn anything new, or worse, they might believe they know it all already. These mindsets can get them even *more* stuck because they'll never make enough money to ditch their day jobs.

With the right skills—*marketable* skills—*virtually anyone* can build work-from-anywhere income. Like I said, I've never met anyone who couldn't build work-from-anywhere income—just people who didn't. If you can read this book, you can achieve true work-from-anywhere independence.

Yes; that's really it. You don't need a different job. You don't need a better boss. You don't even need a bigger raise. You just need *marketable* skills. Mo' skills = mo' money. It's kind of my life's mantra!

So if you're high in the marketable-skills department, that's wonderful news. I'm going to show you how to market those skills so you can earn income from anywhere (Be sure to send pics!) If you don't know whether you have a marketable skill to sell, let me reassure you that *you do.* You can start with the skills you have. It might not make you a ton of money at first, but that's no reason to worry either—because increasing your income is simple too. Just improve or add to your skills. Mo' skills = mo' money, remember? Don't forget it.

Also, don't believe the lie that you need a new or better degree before you start. You don't! This book will push you to find your hidden, marketable, and potentially high-paying skills—the stuff you might be taking for granted. I'll also give you *tons* of resources to continue boosting those skills. Lastly, you'll learn to turn those skills into income. You can even use the 28-day launch plan at the end of this book to build your very own work-from-anywhere freedom. Leave your excuses at the door. You don't need to be a tech genius; you don't need to be a social media rock star. In fact, many successful students *aren't* either of those things.

For example, my former student Stephanie Spillmann thought she had to be super tech-savvy to work at home. Here's how she described her fear.

> **❝**I was honestly scared to try at first since I knew I'd need a website and some marketing and social media skills. I was new to everything business-related online, but I jumped in anyway."

Stephanie didn't let fear stop her. When she started, she didn't have all the skills she needed... but she had some of them, and that was enough. She started *before* she felt ready, and now she's a professional proofreader and blogger. You can see some of her work at HealthySavvyAndWise.com.

Got it? You *don't* have to know everything when you're starting out. That's the good news: There's *nothing* in this book that you *can't* do, and you don't have to know everything to get started. But there's also some potentially bad news. Although making this happen might be simple, it's *not* easy. You need to make a big commitment. That might be bad news for some folks. To make this real, you have to *want* it. Some people say they want a better life for themselves and their family, but they aren't willing to do anything differently to get it. You've got to *do something* if you want this life—this freedom—for yourself. Refuse to let *anything* stand in the way… especially not yourself.

You may have already identified your marketable skill. You could be *completely new* to the concept of work-from-anywhere income. It doesn't matter. **You have the power to turn your life** into whatever you want it to be. I'm here to show you the way, but *you* have to do the work. You don't hold the key; you *are* the key to your own success.

You could read this book seventeen times and memorize every last word, and your life would be exactly the same. There is nothing I can personally do to change your life. Only you can do this. Only you have the power. You have the power to change your whole world—you just need to decide. *Decide* to free your mind of lies. *Decide* to learn powerful skills. *Decide* to take action consistently. *Decide* not to give up. It's all a choice. Your choices can be either your greatest source of power or your biggest weakness. Choose power. Choose *you*.

HOW TO USE THIS BOOK

This book is for action takers. If you bought this book looking for a magic pill for overnight success, you came to the wrong place. On the other hand, if you bought this book looking for a proven roadmap and a swift kick in the butt to get started, you and I were meant to meet. Let's look at how best to use this book so you get the best possible results.

I split this book into two parts. Each of the parts serves an important but different purpose. Here's what you need to know about each part to get the most out of this book.

Part 1 takes you behind the curtain of my personal journey from a 16-year-old supermarket cashier to a millionaire at age 30. I share my ups and downs, my strengths and weaknesses, and my greatest successes and failures. Why am I sharing so much detail with you? Because I know you need to trust me before you'll do what I say. Since I want you to do what I say—take action!—I'm airing a bunch of dirty laundry. Showing you exactly where I started is the most effective way to gain your trust. By the end of Part 1, you'll be confident you can trust me to guide you on your own journey.

Part 2 is your plan. This is where I walk you through the three steps to work-from-anywhere freedom. I'll help you free your mind from the lies that hold people back. Then you'll learn to spot and avoid scams and identify the right work-at-home opportunity for you. Finally, I'll turn you loose on a 28-day, step-by-step launch plan.

Last thing: I come across new tools and resources all the time so I built an exclusive section on my website just for you. It's loaded with the best and latest resources to help you learn the skills—so you can do more than just pay the bills.

You'll find a bunch of ways to connect with me there, too. I'm so excited to be on this journey with you.

RESOURCE PAGE

WorkAtHomeSchool.com/BookResources

PART ONE

Behind the Curtain— From Supermarket to Success

CHAPTER ONE
Will Work for Pay:
My First Attempts at Making Money

Sometimes you need to kiss a few frogs before you find a prince. That was pretty much my relationship with the *normal* working world. I worked from the time I could legally earn my own money. I always surpassed my job requirements, but I *always* got into trouble at work for breaking some rule or pushing back against my bosses. It didn't matter the job; it was only a matter of time before I either jumped ship or got pushed off the edge of the boat.

Looking back, it was obvious what the problem was. I wasn't built to wear a uniform. I wasn't built to sit at a desk all day. I wasn't built to follow rules that make no sense. And I wasn't built to get paid by the hour instead of getting paid for performance. (Is that you, too? Let's be friends.)

I always wanted to be my own boss, work from anywhere, and get paid for what I did—not how long it took me to do it. Don't get me wrong; some of my bosses were just dumb. Some were just *jerks.* It wasn't *all* me. Some of the rules really didn't make any sense, but it didn't matter. I wasn't built to be an employee. It just took me a while to figure that out.

My First Attempt at Making Money

When I turned 16, I started looking for my first job. I applied *everywhere* I could think of, but nobody hired me. I filled out so many paper applications that my hand cramped up on me. Finally, after getting rejected by Chuck E. Cheese, Subway, Boston Market, and dozens of others, I got a job.

It took me five months to land a cashier job with the grocery store, Winn-Dixie—making $5.70 per hour! It even took a hookup through a friend's older brother to land *that* job. That's right. It took a personal connection to get a $5.70-per-hour job as a grocery store cashier.

That's okay; I had a job, and I learned a lot about myself there. The most valuable lesson came from winning a bread-selling contest. As strange as that sounds, it showed me how much better it is to get paid for performance instead of by the hour. Our bosses had challenged the cashiers to sell loaves of bread—they dangled 10 extra hours of pay for the winner. Highly motivated, I sold so much bread that my managers got annoyed with me. Why? Because they kept having to refill my bread basket!

I stayed at Winn-Dixie long enough to score an, erm... *generous* pay bump to $6.38 per hour. Then my friend Chris told me about a hotel receptionist gig that would pay me a whopping $7.50 per hour. At 17 years old, not only was that a pretty decent raise, it was also a move to my dream job at the time. No joke; I thought being a hotel receptionist was the coolest job in the world. I could wear nice outfits and quite literally "hold the keys" to people's vacations. I *loved* the idea of dressing nicely, helping people enjoy a few days of their lives, and making an extra $1.12 per hour. I skipped school for the interview and got the job pretty much on the spot.

Discovering the Hospitality World Wasn't So Hospitable to Me

The receptionist gig was fun for the most part, but I kept butting heads with management over the smallest things. I stuck around for a little more than a year and got reprimanded a few times—mostly because my dream of wearing nice outfits turned out to be mistaken. We were required to wear these ugly polo shirts paired with some *ridiculous* company-issued high-waisted work pants. The zipper was about as long as my forearm. There was *no way* I was wearing those, so I did the most logical, charitable thing I could think of: I donated those pants to Goodwill immediately. I bought a cute, modern pair of dress pants in the same color and wore those instead. Nobody noticed for a few months… but once they did, they acted like I had killed my manager's puppy. They gave me two new pairs of the hotel-issued variety and made me wear them on threat of termination. *Whatever.* I looked and felt like an idiot, but it was their hotel so I sucked it up. I mean… if they wanted a dorky-looking receptionist versus a far more sophisticated one, that was on them. So I wore those ugly pants until I was able to jump ship to another hotel.

Although I got paid a whopping 50 cents more per hour, the next place wasn't much better. I just couldn't deal with my boss. I was 18; my boss was just two years older and was power trippin' like *whoa*. She enjoyed every ounce of power she got from the hotel, too. As a rebel at heart, I could barely stand it. It was *not* a good mix.

By this point, I was starting to see a trend. *I didn't like getting bossed around.* I especially didn't like getting bossed around by people I thought were unqualified. I also had to do a bunch of things I didn't think made much sense, but I played the game as long as I could and then got out of there, too.

One More Try

My next stop was an animal hospital. Again, it seemed like a cool gig, but so many of their rules made no sense to me. For example, on Wednesdays I was the only one at the office, and my only job was to answer the phones. It didn't matter how slow it was—I wasn't allowed to do *anything* but sit and wait for the phone to ring. Of course, I didn't just sit there and answer the phones. Come on; I'm all about efficiency! Between calls, I wrote papers, read books for school, and studied. If anyone popped in, I'd make myself look busy, but that's about it.

If that wasn't bad enough, my boss (the vet) *chewed me out* one day for something that never happened. One of our clients told the vet that I'd suggested we were going to euthanize his cat at his appointment. Seriously. Here's what *really* happened. A guy called the office crying. He told me he thought his cat needed to get put down. I acted sympathetically and helped him make an appointment to come in to see the vet. In his mind, I told him, "Come in, and we'll kill your cat tomorrow." I *actually* said something to the effect of, "I'm so sorry. The doctor can see you tomorrow. Why don't you come in then?"

It was clearly a simple miscommunication—no one's fault—yet my boss *tore* into me. I sat there and took it. That was a turning point for me. I was *done* with that place.

Putting My Money Where My Mouth Was

I resented all the wasted time I spent at a desk doing nothing of real value. I never really felt like the people telling me what to do knew what they were doing.

I always felt like my destiny was for something more than that. I wanted to do my own thing and live by my own rules... or by no rules at all. I'd had enough. I lasted six months at the vet job before I couldn't take it anymore and left. And I needed to do something big. I decided to take a year abroad and finally start experiencing the world on my own terms. My family was from Germany, so I decided to go there.

I had saved up $70,000. That was thanks in part to my Oma (German for *grandma*)—who'd helped me open my first savings account at age 7—my frugal living habits, and working hard. It was time to put my money where my mouth was. I tried to get some scholarships to fund the trip, which didn't pan out—but it didn't matter. Nothing would stop me.

CHAPTER TWO
The Awakening

I t was October of 2007. A few weeks into my stay at the University of Koblenz in Germany, I got my first paying gig as a proofreader for a professor in the English department. It paid me 110 Euros per month—regardless of whether they had any work for me or not. I'm a bit of a word nerd, so it was a perfect fit.

I also got a second gig for 12 Euros per hour to help a young Ukrainian businessman practice his English. All I needed to do was meet the guy in a coffee shop and talk with him. It was a pretty easy and fun gig.

Those two gigs taught me a lot about myself. I had no idea what lay ahead for me… but I did know that I loved working with words, earning income from anywhere, and not having a boss.

The plot thickened!

Back to Reality with a New Identity

When my year in Germany was over, I had a really hard time getting back into the swing of things at home. I had so much fun and enjoyed so much freedom in Germany. It felt like I'd teleported from one existence and one identity to another. I'll never forget walking back into my room the night I got home and seeing my wall calendar still open to the same month *a year ago*. It was surreal; like the life I'd known had stopped for a while and now I had to reconnect with it. But I was a different person who had experienced a different world and no matter how hard I tried, I couldn't just go back to my old life.

It frustrated me that none of my friends would ever fully understand that experience. To them, my time in Germany was just a vacation. So many people frustrated me beyond belief, asking the incessant and vague "How was your trip?" questions. In my mind— nay, in my *reality*—my year abroad was not a "trip" at all. It was my life. It was the life I wanted to live.

Avoiding Another "Real" Job

I had burned through about $12,000 of my savings while I was away, so I wanted to make some money. I started looking for freelance proofreading jobs to see if I could replicate what I had done in Germany. I did a little bit of work for a debt-consolidation company and started tutoring college and high school students in German for between $12.50 and $17.50 per hour. As I got more students, I began charging $20 and sometimes $30 per hour. I even got hired to translate German university transcripts for an exchange student once. My $20 to $30 per hour was a far cry from the $8.50

per hour I was making before going to Germany one year earlier. Things were looking up!

Funny enough, I didn't even know the work I was doing was considered "freelancing." I was just looking for gigs to pay me so I could avoid another stupid job with another stupid boss. I also hadn't been freelancing long enough to know whether I could make it my full-time, permanent career path. I was still stuck in the mindset that I needed to finish college and find a "real job." Picturing myself working any job I looked into made me sick to my stomach, though...

Forcing Myself to Get a "Real Job" Anyway

I kept proofreading and tutoring but also took a $12-per-hour receptionist position working at a busy and prestigious court reporting agency. My workload was intense and never-ending. I answered the phones, replied to company emails, and dealt with incoming clients. I cleaned conference rooms. I scanned and filed paperwork. I did data entry. I sorted all the mail. I did *all* the things and some days, I couldn't get it all done no matter how hard I tried.

It was the first time I had ever *not* totally crushed productivity expectations at a job, so I was frustrated. I worked as quickly and efficiently as I could, but their business was growing fast and I just couldn't keep up! My boss couldn't understand why the person who had the job before me got all *their* work done, though. I tried to explain there was more work because of the company's obvious— and intended!—growth. I also told her how much time I was spending correcting the last receptionist's mistakes, but she didn't care. She wanted everything she demanded to get done. The constant pressure to do more and more caused me to spend all day every day paranoid I'd get fired at any moment.

I decided to suck it up and "play the game" as long and as well as I could, but it kept getting worse. I even got reprimanded once about the cheese I ordered for a company party. Apparently, the cheese I ordered didn't look "artisanal" enough to suit the boss lady's fancy. Seriously. This was the kind of stuff I was dealing with.

I totally should've gotten outta Dodge, but I was 22 years old, fresh out of college, and green to the business world. I had no idea what it was like to work in a positive environment. In fact, I thought that was just how "prestigious" downtown businesses operated. Plus, I had moved out of my parents' house to rent a room for $425 per month plus utilities. I didn't want to dip into savings to pay for that, so in my mind I had no other choice but to keep grinding it out.

No matter how unreasonable that lady was, they couldn't deny I was getting a ton done. It would have taken two of me to do everything they wanted me to do (for $12 per hour). Six months later, I got a $2-per-hour raise. I celebrated by spending 17-and-a-half-hours' worth of that raise on a $35 bottle of wine to celebrate with Ben, my then-boyfriend (now husband, yay!). Clearly, I'm a word nerd, not a numbers gal. If I had realized how much of my raise I spent on that bottle, I'd have picked out a $3 bottle at Walmart instead—and probably a second one to drink at work!

I kept getting raises and promotions there. I got a second raise to $15 per hour six months later—plus a promotion to marketing coordinator. By January 2011, I was at $16 per hour and had business cards with the fancy title of "Director of Marketing and Business Development" on them. I was in charge of building a team of marketing coordinators—a fancy term for salespeople, as I would soon learn.

Bait and Switch

Once again, the "real world" proved to be a nightmare for me. I worked my butt off for years... just to make $16 per hour. Something wasn't adding up. I started to catch on that I wouldn't be getting anywhere worthwhile anytime soon. Relying on one-dollar-per-hour raises wasn't going to cut it. Working for other people and having to weather through all their pettiness and personal issues was pretty miserable too. With my latest promotion, I was hoping I'd finally have *some* control and just a *little* flexibility. Not so fast.

My fancy title was simply a way to make me do more work. And I still needed to do everything *their* way—even if it made no sense. I wasn't allowed to do any real *marketing*. All they wanted me and "my team" to do was make cold calls all day. That was *not* marketing; that was sales, which was not what I was hired to do. Even worse, if we finished our list of leads early, we had to get leads from slower workers and make their calls.

Productivity wasn't rewarded. Quite the opposite: It felt like a punishment to be efficient. People caught on. The volume of work you actually completed didn't matter. You only needed a submissive attitude and (mostly) error-free work to get your paycheck. If you didn't finish your work, then more efficient people (like me) would finish it for you—so there was *zero* incentive for most employees to do anything more than the bare minimum.

I also learned that all the other managers were salaried and had an extra week of paid vacation. In fact, when I asked for three weeks off for my wedding and honeymoon, they made me feel like I owed them big time. For the rest of the year, they made me feel like a horrible person if I needed even just a few hours off to get my teeth cleaned!

I was nothing but a hard-working, low-paid puppet. I'd grown to really, really hate it there. I hated everything about it. I hated forcing my team into *sales* when they were hired to do *marketing*. I hated that I wasn't given the same privileges as the other managers. I hated doing more work than others for the same pay just because I was more efficient than them.

Most of all, I hated I had to spend the best nine hours of every weekday sitting on a *bar stool* chained to my work area. If you're going to make me sit on a bar stool, at least serve me some drinks!

They were *militant* about time, too. If we clocked in at 8:02 a.m., we'd get in trouble. If we clocked out one minute before 5:00 p.m., we'd get in trouble. They *owned* us from 8:00 a.m. until 5:00 p.m. every day. That place was the worst. It was only a matter of time before it all blew up... not very much time, either.

The Rebellion

At that point, I stopped even *trying* to play the game and started rebelling. It was pointless. The best I could hope for was a small raise once a year, so I decided I was *done* doing other people's work.

It only took me three or four hours to finish my day's work, so that's all they were going to get from me. I'd get my work done in the first three or four hours of the day, and then I quietly did *whatever I wanted* until 5:00 p.m. when I was allowed to go home.

I still got more done than anyone else in the first half of my day. I always made sure I got all my work done; I simply wasn't going to keep working harder and harder just to get nothing but other people's work in return.

I eventually allowed my "marketing" team members to do the same thing. I told them as long as they got their work done—without errors—I didn't care how they managed the rest of their time. They were getting paid an even lower wage than me, so it was fine with me if they got their work done faster and filled their remaining time how they wanted.

As a result, our productivity didn't suffer. Our accuracy didn't suffer. Not surprisingly, my policy incentivized my team to *perform* because they could earn more free time. That resulted in a significant boost in everyone's happiness. Our department had the highest morale in the office.

I still got so much done every day that the operations manager adored me. She didn't know—and never asked—how long it took me. I *always* earned a quarterly bonus and scored high on my performance reviews. Everything was going fine until somebody decided to check how I was spending my time.

When "It" Finally Hit the Fan

The company bought software that constantly recorded everyone's computer activities. I knew they used it, but I wasn't worried. Part of me knew it would take a while for them to suspect anything because of my high productivity and my team's positivity. But another part of me actually *hoped* they'd figure it out. That way, I'd either be able to prove my point about productivity... or they'd fire me. I was fine either way.

It took them more than five months to check up on me. Once they did, all hell broke loose. Upper management spent *two full days* locked in an office together. For two days, they printed more than 1,000 pages of what they called "evidence" of my "criminal activity." They even covered up the windows so nobody could see what they were up to. For a group of people so concerned about the best use of company time, they sure wasted a lot of it themselves those two days!

When they confronted me, they said I had been "stealing time" from the company and fired me. Within two days, I went from being everybody's favorite to fired—like *ugly* fired. The owner of the company called me a thief and told me I was a "worthless pig" who would die alone. One of the other managers said I shouldn't have children because I had no morals. And those are just the highlights—or lowlights, depending on your perspective!

The whole office was told I was fired for stealing. My sister-in-law accidentally emailed me at my work email address after I got fired, and the operations manager replied to tell her they fired me for theft. Not only was that not true, it's also considered defamation—which is not only mean; it's *illegal* in Florida!

It gets worse. The owner demanded I pay her $2,000 or she'd sue me for breaking some sort of law. I chalked that up to her wanting to hurt me on the way out. There's no other explanation I could think of. She was a 60-something woman who drove a brand-new Cadillac Escalade. Her agency was growing fast largely because of the work I'd done for her. She didn't need my $2,000.

Whatever. I wrote her a check and moved on with my life. I hated working for other people. I hated policies that didn't make sense. I hated my commute. I hated dealing with demanding and unreasonable bosses. I hated that the prize for performance wasn't more money, but more work for the same money. And I hated making cold sales calls.

I just wanted to get out of there. A few weeks later, I shared my story with a friend who's an employment attorney. What I learned from her shocked me: She said the owner's $2,000 money grab on my way out was actually *extortion*. What I did wasn't criminal theft. I didn't break a law; I just broke company rules. I got all my work done and they were happy with me. They only cared once they saw how fast I was getting it done.

Apparently, I could have sued my old boss—but I didn't. I didn't know it yet, but my success following this epic "failure" would become the sweetest form of revenge imaginable.

Here's the Thing...

Obviously the extortion thing took it too far, but my ex-boss was absolutely right in firing me. I would've fired me, too. I broke the rules. I didn't like the rules, but they were the rules, and I broke them. I get it.

As I sat there listening to my boss call me a sack of trash, I knew I would *never* let anything like that happen again. I would *never* depend on someone else giving me a "job" for the source of all my income. Any success I had in the future would be completely up to me.

I'm not proud of the way I handled things and spent several years after that hating myself for it. I was pretty bored and very unhappy at the court reporting company, but I didn't handle it well. I should've just quit, but I didn't. I passive-aggressively tried to make my workload match my paycheck and broke the company's rules in doing so. While I disagreed with the rule, it was still a rule.

I felt guilty about it for a long time—I even had nightmares for years about the situation. Now that I've stopped kicking myself about my mistakes, I embrace them. I learn from them. *Everyone makes mistakes.*

I openly share my mistakes here not because I'm proud of them, but because I want to help you get past *your* mistakes. There is life beyond that stupid thing you did 5, 10, 20, or 30+ years ago. It's safe to move forward. *Now.* You don't need anyone's permission to do it, either.

My mistakes are now a central part of my message as a blogger and influencer. I hit rock bottom in my sad excuse for a career on August 8, 2011, and that's *exactly* what needed to happen to get me on a path to creating my own success.

Now I consider getting fired as the best thing that has ever happened to me. Why? Because it got me started on the journey that got me where I am today. If you've been fired too, then I want you to know that you can move past it. It's *not* too late. You *didn't* ruin your life. Hire yourself—and fire the ridiculous notion that you need someone else to give you the privilege of creating income. You don't. It's all you, and that's a beautiful thing.

CHAPTER THREE
From Fired to Freelancing

W orking at the court reporting agency wasn't all bad. I proofread a lot of the court reporters' transcripts, which opened the door for me to start a side hustle as a freelance proofreader. By the time I got fired, I had built up that side-hustle income to about $400 per month.

Three years later, I launched the award-winning blog Proofread Anywhere. Currently it's home to two online courses that help people with eagle eyes turn their skills into income. Unbeknownst to me, Proofread Anywhere would become massively successful—both for me and my students.

I took to blogging like a fish takes to water. My skills developed rapidly, and at this point, you know what having mo' skills means: mo' money. My business evolved and expanded and now generates multiple millions of dollars in annual revenue. Before you scoff, roll your eyes, or dismiss my success as pure luck, you need to know it wasn't a straight arrow up from $400 per month to millions per year! In fact, after getting fired back in 2011 I shelled out $7,000 of my savings to become a personal trainer... only to realize I didn't like personal training. Ha! Ultimately I realized that no matter what I was doing, I'd be miserable as long as I had a set schedule, commute, and limited income.

I needed freedom I could only have if I created it myself. I couldn't take another day job. I wouldn't deal with unreasonable bosses, stupid rules, or life-sucking commutes anymore. I wouldn't settle for limited earning potential, either. Somehow, I was going to create the income—and life—I wanted.

I didn't know it yet, but I already had the only two things I needed to make it happen: marketable skills and a willingness to take action.

Slowly Finding My Freedom

Even after graduating from personal training school, I kept gravitating back to proofreading. I'd kept two proofreading clients the whole time and loved doing it. The work came easily, and the pay was good.

I averaged $30 per hour working from home as a proofreader. It was helpful to have side income to beef up my savings. I had $500 deposits coming in here and there on the regular, but for some reason, I still felt I needed a "real" job to make "real" money. I had never considered the possibility that I could turn my side hustle into my primary income. It kind of snuck up on me when it happened!

In July 2012, I landed a remote gig with another court reporting agency as a proofreader. I kept getting more and more work from them. To keep up, I needed to innovate ways to work more efficiently—and that's when the switch flipped.

The faster I worked, the more transcripts I could proofread. The more transcripts I could proofread, the more money I could earn. It was just like in the old days of selling loaves of warm bread at Winn-Dixie, only the prize was much bigger. So I started looking for ways to hack my proofreading process to work smarter and faster. For example, I started proofreading using an iPad. A paperless process allowed me to work digitally and avoid spending time printing and scanning transcript pages.

Within two months of landing that gig, freelance proofreading became my primary income. By the end of 2012, I was making more money proofreading than I made at my old job. Even better, I was working an average of 25 hours per week. I worked 45 hours per week at my old job—not including commute time. In 2013, I earned $47,000 proofreading. I earned another $43,000 proofreading in 2014. Personal training quickly got demoted to my side hustle, and eventually I stopped the personal training altogether.

The work was more enjoyable than both my day job and personal training, too. I worked from home, usually on the couch—but sometimes in bed! No more rush-hour traffic or set schedules. It became even clearer that the traditional working world wasn't for me. It didn't matter what I did. If I had a commute and a set schedule of any kind, it was only a matter of time before I lost my mind.

With proofreading, I had deadlines, but that's about it. I could wear whatever I wanted. I could work from wherever I wanted. As long as I got the work done well and on time, my clients were happy. I was happy, too—I was taking back my life!

Building My Multimillion-Dollar Business

By November 2014, I knew proofreading was going to be my primary income. Over the years, I'd helped quite a few people get started as a freelance proofreader—and people constantly asked me about it—so I decided to start a blog. That's when I bought the domain ProofreadAnywhere.com. I had no idea what I was doing, but I started sharing everything I could on the site to help people.

I had very little confidence that I'd actually stick to this new project—like many people, I had a track record of giving up when things got tough. I also had almost no confidence that anyone would want to read my blog at all. The mere thought that someone would ever pay me to teach them anything was even crazier. I decided to give it a go anyway. If things weren't going well after six months or so, I thought, then I could quit.

At first, I only planned to do two things. First, I'd write about my life and what it was like to be able to work from home on an iPad. Second, I'd sell an eBook I created. I called it How to Make Money Proofreading Transcripts for Court Reporters. Creative name, I know... and I had no idea that little blog and eBook would turn into something so big.

My First—and Worst—Online Product

Too many people think you need to be perfect to make money, but I'm living proof that isn't true. If you don't believe me, head on over to the Resources page (WorkAtHomeSchool.com/BookResources) to see the front cover of the train wreck that was my first eBook. You need to see the beautiful mint green Microsoft Word cover to fully appreciate it.

It took me about four days to write that eBook. I had a friend proofread it. Everyone who writes needs someone else to proofread their writing. The writer needs to concentrate on being creative and delivering the right information. Even I use proofreaders!

My proofreader missed a ton of errors, but that's okay. It was ugly and imperfect, but I knew those 30 pages had everything anyone needed to know to be successful as a proofreader. So I did what any completely naïve baby marketer would do... I started selling it. I offered a full training program containing the eBook, a test transcript, an answer key, and personalized feedback from me on their work—for $150. That was a steal compared to the money my students could make with the skill, yet I felt super guilty charging for my program! Seventeen brave people apparently thought the full training program was worth it, though. Eventually I learned that nearly everyone feels guilty about charging for something they used to do for free.

Unfortunately, things didn't exactly go according to plan from there. Most of the people who bought the training, read the eBook, and did the work responded positively. But it was a lot more work than I expected... my students had a lot of questions.

At first, I couldn't believe they couldn't figure things out from what I'd written. I figured they could just "read between the lines." Later, I realized the questions they asked were as valuable to me as my answers were to them. People started stumbling into the gigantic holes that I hadn't realized were in the eBook. All of the questions they asked translated into opportunities for me to make my product better.

If you're ever feeling discouraged, head on back to the Resources page. Have another look at the cover of the eBook that started it all. Remember, I turned that into a business generating more than $200,000 per month in sales in less than three years. If I—a total newbie with no tech skills—can turn a crappy eBook into a multi-million-dollar business, imagine what you could do if you start and refuse to give up!

When I share this story with people, occasionally someone will tell me it was foolish to put out such a crappy product—especially when people see the picture of the cover! Some folks say I should have made the product perfect before publishing it. Here's the thing: If you wait for a product to be perfect to start selling it, you'll never sell it. Why? Because it'll never be perfect.

Also, until you start selling your product, you'll never know where the holes are. You can't find all the holes in your product just by having your bestie look it over. To find the holes, you must be brave enough to let people fall into them. Find people who are interested in your topic, who've invested time and money, and who will actually implement what they learn. Their questions reveal the holes. So if writing a how-to book like I did is on your horizon, let people read your book. Let them use your product. It's scary, but doing scary things is how we grow!

CHAPTER FOUR
Turning Freelancing into Freedom

That first eBook turned into an online course that launched in February 2015. I faced many fears. I did things my own way. I learned as I went along... and I totally crushed it.

We started with a subscriber list of just 220 people—most of whom I knew personally. In the first 90 days, the blog generated more than $130,000 in revenue. That was more money than I had made the previous three years *combined*. I couldn't believe I generated it with my first online course in only three *months*.

Imagine for a moment that I'd given up after just a few weeks—or the first time things got difficult. What if I'd never gotten started at all? I almost didn't, you know. I used excuses like, "It's too hard!" and "I don't know how!" as reasons to not learn. Too many people use lack of knowledge, bumps in the road, bad feedback, or past mistakes as reasons to give up (or never start at all). Don't let that be you! *The only way you can fail is if you give up.*

That initial success with the blog was all the proof I needed: I would never have to depend on an employer for income ever again. All I needed to do was keep developing my skills.

In the Beginning, There Was Doubt

Despite my success—and my certainty that I'd never have a boss again—I still didn't fully believe it was possible to earn more than $40,000 a year on a regular basis. Although I'd just created $130,000 in income doing something really cool, it still seemed unreal.

Since then, I've learned that self-doubt is the newbie's curse. Just about every one of us wonders, "Can I *really* do this?" I did. Almost every person I've helped asks me that question, too.

My self-doubt sounded a lot like, "Is this kind of life even possible for someone like me? I got fired from my last 'real' job!" Then I wondered, "If it is possible, should I do what everyone else is doing? Should I follow a process? Should I figure things out on my own?"

I couldn't open the computer without seeing some *expert* shouting at me about how to make money online. And they almost all said to do something different. It was so overwhelming that I just shut 'em all out.

That was a wise move, in retrospect. Many new entrepreneurs become so paralyzed by those voices. Many get stuck in the perpetual "research loop" trying to figure out what to do and who to learn from. Either way, they *never* end up actually doing anything. I've met people who have bounced from expert to expert without any progress. I've seen people buy course after course with nothing to show for it, in some cases for *years*.

But I had generated $130,000 in revenue in *90 days!* That kind of success does things to a person. I thought about quitting while I was ahead. I wondered whether I had reached the top and it was all downhill from there. It felt like I was riding a wave that could crash without notice. People close to me voiced similar concerns—and I had attracted some haters as well.

One of my biggest fears was that everything the haters said about me was true. Maybe I really didn't have any business trying to help people make money. Maybe I didn't have what it took to be a successful blogger. Maybe it really was only a matter of time before I'd crash and burn.

I was scared. But even when I felt like a total fraud on the brink of failure, I didn't give up. I kept learning. I kept doing what felt authentic to me. I kept doing what would help the most people. In spite of my fear, I kept moving forward. The fear fueled my fire toward continued success for both me and my growing tribe of students. I adopted an "I'll show 'em!" attitude toward the haters and naysayers in my life.

And, well... I showed 'em.

Fast.

Growth, Growth, and Even More Growth

In April 2015, I told my proofreading clients I was going on vacation. I took a week-long trip to New York City with a friend I'd met in Germany. I even made an appearance on *The Dr. Oz Show* while I was there!

While I was gone, my blog generated 18 sales of my online course. I made about $11,000 while on *vacation!*

When I got back, I decided to officially retire from freelancing and focus on my online business. I told my clients I would no longer be proofreading. I felt so *free!* To have earned that much money in only a *few months* as opposed to an entire year was a *big deal*. It was enough for me to take the leap of faith and move into my online business full-time.

By the end of May 2015, the blog had generated more than $100,000. Ben and I decided to pay off the fifteen-year mortgage on our two-bedroom house—nine years early. Writing a $59,000 check never felt so good.

With my new complete location independence, Ben and I decided to travel for a year. So in July 2015, we packed up our furniture, rented out our house to tenants, and traveled around South America. We spent time in Ecuador, Peru, Bolivia, Argentina, Chile, and Uruguay. For our five-year wedding anniversary, we even went off the grid for a two-week cruise that took us from Santiago, Chile around the horn of South America all the way to Buenos Aires, Argentina. We could see Antarctica from our balcony!

By May 2016—just 15 months after I launched my first course—revenue reached $1 million. I was 29. Just shy of a year later, total assets reached $1 million, officially making me a millionaire at age 30.

We returned home from our travels in July 2016. A few weeks later, we closed on a half-acre piece of property in Winter Park, the wealthiest city in Central Florida. We even hired an architect to design our dream house on the lot. All of that was possible thanks to money we earned while traveling around South America for a year.

Was That It?

For more than two years, the only thing I offered was a single course. I wondered if that was *it* for me. I had made more money during those two years than I would have in *two decades* at the court reporting agency. Part of me believed I had reached the peak. Just like last time, though, I hadn't. Apparently, the sky's the limit if you put people first. My life's mission was to teach as many people as possible *real* skills they can use to earn *real* money from home— and there was no end in sight for that mission!

In the two years I had been in business, many people had asked me to create a course for other types of proofreading. They wanted to proofread less technical stuff than legal transcripts. I brushed it off, made excuses, and allowed my self-limiting beliefs to convince me I couldn't do it. Plus, as free as I was to travel the world and even go off the grid for weeks at a time, I was still doing a lot of the work myself. I had *some* help but not enough to take the time to build a second course.

By December 2016, I had built a solid management and marketing team for my business. That's when something clicked. I could breathe. I had help with the business side of things and could be creative again. So my team and I put our heads together and made the course on general proofreading a reality!

It was the first major addition to our curriculum after our initial course. We put a lot of work into it, and even though my audience had specifically asked for that second course, it was scary. *What if no one bought it?* I wondered. *Even worse, what if they did, but no one liked it and I damaged my reputation?*

Are you seeing the pattern with my mindset? I had the *same* menacing thoughts surrounding this new course that I had before launching my first one. It didn't matter that I had sold over $1 million worth of proofreading courses. It didn't matter that I had helped *thousands* of people make money from home. I went right back to my default: *major* self-doubt.

By that time, though, I knew enough to ignore those thoughts and plow full steam ahead. Those feelings of self-doubt always come back—I've learned to expect them and welcome them. I now know that fear *never* goes away; it just changes its outfit... and *we* get better at taking action no matter how scary the outfit gets. Look at fear as a tool to gauge your potential for growth. If the thing you want to do isn't scary at all, then you're not going to grow from it. If it's easy, then you won't learn anything new. Good things happen when you act in spite of fear. Facing fear always makes us stronger.

It's Your Turn...

I may have earned a lot of money freelancing. I may have helped others do the same, too. But I'm the same as most people when it comes to those fears. I started out earning money the same way almost everyone does. I'm *not* smarter than you. I'm *definitely not* cooler than you. I have no magic wand or secret sauce, and I've made some flat-out *embarrassing* mistakes. I'm human. Just like you. In other words, the only difference between you and me is what I've *done*, not who I am.

For the rest of the book, I'm going to teach you the most important things I've learned on my rocky path to success. I'll share the biggest lessons I learned from building my multimillion-dollar business. I'll share the best tips and strategies I've got—the very same mindsets and strategies that have pushed me and thousands of others out of our comfort zones and into a world of freedom.

If you follow all the steps, you can start making money from home or anywhere else you choose—but it takes all the steps.

You *must* break free from the lies about money, education, work, business, and success. If you skip this step, your very own mind will cause you to give up when you hit a bump in the road.

You can't skip leveling up. Once you throw out the garbage, you've got to replace it with gold: empowering beliefs plus new-and-improved skills. If you skip this step, you *might* be able to make some money, but chances are you'll be struggling financially, full of doubt, and still susceptible to scams. You might even find yourself building a business that makes you *miserable.*

A common mistake people make is feeling stuck with whatever they choose. That's what leads to misery. Of course it's important not to choose something you hate just because you want to make money, but it's also not a good idea to spend a ton of time hemming and hawing over finding the "perfect" thing you'll do forever. You never know where the journey will take you, so the important thing is to find something that works—for now—and just start.

That's the final step: Launch your business. Start! For most people, that means starting before you feel "ready." You don't get traction without action! You can't build momentum before you start moving. It's a law of physics or something... really!

Ready to unlock the wonderful world of work-from-*anywhere* income?

On to Part 2!

PART TWO

3 Steps to Work-From-Anywhere Freedom

Step 1:
Free Your Mind from the Lies
that Hold You Back

CHAPTER FIVE
Why These Lies Hold You Back

The biggest obstacle you'll face in your work-at-home journey is freeing your mind from *lies* you've believed your whole life. Many of us grow up learning dangerous things about money, education, work, and business or success. Those things are often meant to help us... but end up holding us back instead. They put us on an endless path of job hopping and limited income.

If we don't recognize the lies for what they are and make the choice to stop believing them, we'll waste time, money, and likely never achieve the freedom we crave. For example, we're told we need to go to school, get a college degree—or two, or three—no matter what it costs. We're told that education (mere information) is the key to earning income. Then we're told we need to sit in traffic or on a bus or train twice a day to go to "work." We're told to accept getting paid *just* enough to keep up with our bills. We're told to "just be happy to have a job" when we're working ourselves half to death for a boss who can take away our income at any moment.

If that sounds familiar, you're not alone. That's what it was like for me at the hotels, the animal hospital, and the court reporting agency. I worked my butt off for between $7 and $16 per hour. It didn't matter how fast I worked. It didn't matter how well I performed. The most I could hope for was a one-dollar-per-hour raise every six months to a year—if that. Money was hard to come by. Money doesn't grow on trees, they told me. It's a *limited resource* with only so much to go around. If I earned more money, there would be less for others. I could expect *incremental* raises, at best. *Exponential* income growth was impossible. That's how it works… that's what I was *taught*.

For the first two decades of our lives, we're programmed to think we need some kind of formal declaration of our worthiness to make money and enter the workforce. When we look for traditional jobs, a degree means we're worthy. *But that's a lie.* Most people don't need degrees to be successful; they just need in-demand skills—and in this day and age, a fancy degree isn't necessary to acquire skills.

In traditional jobs, our paychecks compensate us for our *time,* not our *productivity.* Nowhere was this more obvious than my last job at the court reporting agency. It wasn't my hourly pay that made this clear, though—it was the fact that my boss told me I was *stealing* from the company by not asking for more work when I'd finished mine. They often got *more* work from me that they got from others, but because I did it in less time, I was *stealing* and the others were good employees.

Lies. This is not how work *has to be*, and even though many workplaces still operate using that antiquated system, things are changing rapidly. Still, these are *tough* lies to get past because they've been so deeply programmed into our brains. For example, many people struggle to price their services when starting up their freelance businesses. They're so used to thinking in terms of time ("It only took me an hour!") that they don't even consider the *value* they served up in that time. We've got to flip the switch on that way of thinking. Time is no longer your measuring stick. *Value* is king.

What other lies do many of us believe? That business and personal lives are two different things. That we're "successful" when we sell the most bread for a supermarket chain. That we're "successful" when we get promoted—even if it's to a meaningless puppet position. That $1-per-hour annual raises are acceptable or even generous. That having two weeks of paid vacation per year is all we get until we retire at 65. That even if we're *miserable*, we should just be happy to have a job at all "in this economy." That it's the economy's fault we're not making more money.

There are so many lies. So many. But the lie I believe sabotages more people than *any* of the others is that *successful people never fail.* The most successful people in the world have failed more times than they can count. I know I have! The difference between people who succeed and people who fail is simple, though. Successful people just never give up. People who fail often never really failed; they just gave up. They stopped trying, while the successful people refused defeat.

Success is subjective, too. Nobody's definition of success but your own matters. That's the beauty of this world—you can design your business around what success means to *you*. Some people will never *feel* successful if they have to commute in a used Honda for two hours a day. Some people won't *feel* successful sitting in the same chair in the same building every day. Others don't care so much about driving. They might even enjoy going to the same office every day—as long as they can wear whatever they want to work. Everybody's different.

For me, success has little to do with money. It's when I'm living my truest life. Summed up with a quote from Henry David Thoreau, "Our truest life is when we are in dreams awake." For many of us, money isn't the dream—*freedom* is the dream. We don't want to be stuck; we want to *choose* how we live our lives. My other favorite quote about success comes from the late and great American journalist Christopher Morley. He said, "There is only one success: to be able to spend your life in your own way." So whatever your dreams are—however you want to live your life—when your choices make that a reality, *that* is success.

Over the next four chapters, I'm going into more detail on the lies that hold people back, and I'll shine an annoyingly bright light on every single one of 'em. It is *so* important you pay attention to these chapters because you'll *never* make your dream life a reality if you let antiquated or just plain *false* beliefs hold you back. It's time to take out the garbage. There is life-changing power when you choose to believe the *truth* instead of lies. And it *is* a choice.

If you believe money is a limited resource in the world, you'll never achieve true financial freedom. You might think there's not enough money for *you* and stop trying. You might believe you're *taking from someone else* every time you earn more money. Either way, you'll hold yourself back. After all, you're a nice person—you don't want to take money out of someone else's pocket, right? People who feel this way about money sabotage themselves. Money isn't a non renewable resource. There's more than enough to go around; I promise!

If you believe you need a formal degree and ceremony to be worthy of a higher income, you'll *never* succeed. If you think you need an MBA to be a business owner, you'll *never* build your freelancing into a business the size of mine. You'll be too timid. You'll lack confidence. Prospective clients will sense that from a mile away. I don't have an MBA, yet I run a multimillion-dollar business. I've said it before and I'll say it again: *I'm not an anomaly.* I've also got a perfectly average IQ. You don't need an expensive degree—nor do you need a genius-level IQ—to learn skills, solve problems, and make money.

If you believe you need to trade time (hours) for money, you'll always have a cap on your income. You'll never break free from your day job, fire your boss, or quit your commute. You might make a few extra bucks a month, but that's about it.

If you believe you should be someone different at work than you are at home, you'll be miserable. A double life will, well… suck the life out of you. I've been there, and you might be there right now. You can be the same person—a skilled, confident, successful and happy person—24/7. *Really.*

Finally, if you believe failure is fatal, that belief could sabotage you. You could give up on your dream way too soon. Even the tiniest roadblock might cause you to pack up and go back to your old life.

Shining the light of truth on these lies is the first step to creating the freedom you want and deserve in your life. You'll *never* achieve true freedom until you *choose* to stop believing lies. Once you do, the other steps are much easier. The other steps are all about what you do after you get out of bed, but breaking free will get you out of bed on days when you "just can't"—because you'll finally know the truth: *you can.*

Ready to take out the trash with me? Here's the truth about money...

CHAPTER SIX
The Truth About Money

Three myths about money keep people from building work-from-anywhere income. We're fed these myths from a young age. We need to rid ourselves from them if we ever want to make real money at home—or from anywhere!

As you work through these, ask yourself whether these myths have held you back. If they have—or if they are currently—be honest with yourself about it. There's power in your actions, and there's power in honesty. The moment we can look at ourselves in the mirror and tell ourselves the truth about how we've been living, we give ourselves the power we need to transform. So commit to telling yourself the truth and doing whatever it takes to train your brain to *believe* that truth. You deserve to live your life that way!

Money Myth No. 1: You're Stuck with a "Fixed Income."

Up until a few years ago, honest to God, I believed that I would never make more than about $40,000 a year. I said that to myself, and I said that to my husband. I said, "Honey, I just don't think I'll ever make more than $40,000 a year, and I guess I'm okay with that because it's enough, y'know?"

And it really *was* enough, mostly because we *made* it be enough by doing less and spending less. We limited our lifestyle to our paychecks. It's not that we weren't *happy* with our lives. We were. I believe we always have the power to be happy regardless of our circumstances, but we *definitely* weren't living our dream life.

I had totally boxed myself into that $40,000 ceiling. I shut down any dream that went beyond that amount. More money felt unrealistic for someone like me. Someone who'd been fired. Someone with a basic degree. I didn't believe I was capable of earning more. That stinkin' thinkin' stuck with me even after I started earning more money. I had convinced myself that, due to "my circumstances," earning more just wasn't an option.

I'd *given* myself a fixed income.

There was no reason I limited myself to $40,000 per year. There was no law saying Caitlin could only earn $40,000 per year. There was nobody confiscating every penny above $40,000 that I earned. It was just *me*. *I* limited myself to that. *I* had convinced *myself* that I'd hit an income ceiling.

A lot of folks in the Work-At-Home Heroes community have the same problem. They believe the myth that there's only so much money coming their way. Every week, I get emails from people with that fixed mindset. Some say they *can't* earn more money. Others say they can't invest in themselves because they're on a "fixed income."

They present it as a Catch-22: I'd love to do more so I can make more, but I'm on a "fixed income" and just *can't*. Here are a few *real*, copied-and-pasted quotes from a few of those emails:

> **❝**Sorry, but I am on a very low fixed income, so the cost of learning the technique to become a proofreader is out of the question!"

———————

"I am on a fixed income and can't afford it."

———————

"The true problem is I flat don't have the money. I understand that the classes are worth it. I am sure they are; however, I am on a very fixed income."

———————

"I'm retired, on a fixed income, struggling to pay rent, and eating Ramen."

———————

"My finances won't allow this as I am on a fixed income presently."

———————

Each of those people saw their income as fixed. Some said the government fixed it. Others said their company or some other source, such as an annuity, fixed it.

Others saw their income as "fixed" but also expressed some hope or desire to change that. Here are some more copied-and-pasted quotes straight from my inbox:

“ *Being on a fixed income, I'd like to 'fix' that."*

_____

"I retired two years ago and have discovered fixed income doesn't fix things."

_____

"Fixed income doesn't always cover the emergencies of life."

_____

Here's the truth. Your *current* income might be set by someone else, but that's only what you're *currently receiving*. There's *no* reason you can't change that. There's *no* reason you can't develop a marketable skill and learn to market that skill to increase your income.

If you're able-minded, "fixed income" is always a choice. Choose to believe this truth. With the right skills and a little help, you can *choose* to make more money. You can choose to reprogram your income thinking. I recommend replacing any fixed-income thinking with the statement, "I write my own income story" from the Work-At-Home Hero Manifesto (see the Preface for the whole thing).

Say it right now—out loud. *I write my own income story.*

How much do you want to earn in a year? $40,000? $80,000? $1,000,000? *More?* The choice is yours. There's work involved no matter the level, but you can choose to do the work it takes to get there. It's a choice… and with choices you have the power to transform.

Don't worry about *how* you're going to make it happen yet. That's why I'm here. Right now the task at hand is to break free from the mindset that your income is fixed. Set a big target that makes you just *a little bit* uncomfortable. Setting a goal too big can backfire just the same as setting a goal too small!

Money Myth No. 2: Making Money is Complicated.

How many times have you heard the cliché "Money doesn't grow on trees"? I've heard it far too many times. The problem isn't that I've found a secret money tree—at least not *literally*. The problem is the phrase implies that it's *complicated* to make money. And that's a myth.

Making money isn't complicated. If you want to make more money, you just need to do a few things differently over and over again. You might not *literally* plant a money tree, but if you develop the right skills and take the right steps, you *can* make money flow your way like a raging river. Skeptical? Stick with me...

People who make money all do two very uncomplicated things. First, they master a skill (with mastery comes confidence). Second, they find people who have problems their skills can solve. See how simple that is? It's *crazy* simple. Yet somehow we manage to overcomplicate it in our society. To earn money, we think we need college; we think we need someone else to give us a job, when in fact, all we need to do is *solve problems for other people.*

Want to make more money than you're making now? You've got two options. You can either increase your productivity to solve more problems in less time, or you can just learn more advanced skills that solve bigger problems! The bigger the problems you can solve, the more money you can make. The cool part is because your brain is always capable of learning more, there is no limit to the skills you can learn (within reason, of course—I, for one, know I'd make a *terrible* rocket scientist). Since there's no limit to the skills you can learn, *there is no limit to the money you can earn!*

That's what I mean when I say you can make money *flow*. When you're starting out, it can feel intimidating—like you're trying to catch fish with a net full of holes! Focus on developing your skills, improving your efficiency, and connecting with people who need your skills. Be consistent and realistic. You're human, and you'll have bad days, but if you don't give up, you literally cannot fail. As you upgrade your skills, your money-fishing net will get stronger and bigger—and you'll catch more money.

Money Myth No. 3: Paying for a College Education is Always a Wise Investment.

Because they believe this myth, intelligent people all over the world will spend up to hundreds of thousands of dollars for a traditional education at a university or college. They'll even take loans to finance it with zero hesitation. They believe they're earning themselves a license to be successful. They think they're paying for job security. But more and more often in this changing economy, we get something much different from success and security on the other side of college. We get mountains of debt. A micromanaging boss who decides how much we get paid and can fire us with no reason. Decades of work before you can retire and do what you *want* to do.

That's the reality we live in. We believe a college education is a wise investment in our future success and security—and for some people, it is! But for the big group of us who just want to make a living to support our families, a college education gave us a poor return on our investment. We have little to show for our time and money output but a $15-per-hour desk job and a load of debilitating debt. A few years into that mess, and we're left wondering: *Is this all there is?*

This experience makes us hesitant to invest in ourselves again later in life. You might be feeling it now. Perhaps it was even a big deal to invest in this book. And maybe now you've made the connection in your mind between your skills and your potential income... but you're hesitant to improve your skills. Why? Because improving your skills costs time and sometimes money, and you're not sure it'll pay off.

I've been there, and I get it. I get emails every day from would-be freelancers who "don't want to spend the money" on a course until they're 100% sure it'll pay off. But it's not *spending* money if you're funneling the money toward something that will increase your income. That's called investing, and as you begin this journey, it's critical to know the difference.

The difference between investing and spending is simple. If you funnel money toward something you *actually use* to grow your income—you're investing. Everything else—fancy office furniture, business books you don't read, new clothes, or anything else that doesn't help you increase your income—is spending. Some people lease expensive cars they can't afford. Some people spend thousands of dollars at spas under the guise of "self-care." Others take luxurious vacations they'll be paying off for years. They justify this spending as *investing in myself.*

I hate to be the bearer of bad news... but that's not investing; that's spending. In fact, that's wasteful spending.

Unlike an expensive car you can't afford, wise investments pay you back over and over (and over!) again. You won't get a return just because you paid for something, though. A positive return on an investment in yourself doesn't depend on any course you pay for or book you bought; it depends on *you.* Information is useless without implementation. Any reputable skills course will work—but only if *you* work. Invest the time to learn, do the work to master the skill, and you'll reap the rewards of higher income.

3 Truths About Money

If you believe these lies about money, you'll never break free from a fixed income. Remember these three truths as you push toward freedom.

First, having a fixed income is a choice for most people. It's not a good thing or a bad thing; it's just a choice you make. You can choose to have a fixed income, and if you're happy with that, fine. If you want more in life than what you can afford right now, you can also choose to allow yourself to dream—and act—bigger. You need no one's permission. You can *choose* to have more if you want it.

Second, making more money isn't complicated. You don't need a company to give you a job. You just need skills that solve other people's problems. If you want to make more money, you need to either solve bigger problems or become more efficient at what you already do. All of this takes work. It's not *easy*, but it is simple. Your brain is not at capacity, so put it to use and see what happens. If you learn new things, you can solve new problems—and make more money!

Third, a good investment actually pays you back over time. An expensive college degree is *not* the end-all, be-all key to success and security. What's the real job security? Your skills. Nobody can take skills away from you. Your brain really is your most powerful tool in earning more income. That's why investing time and/or money in improving your skills is much more likely to give you a positive return on investment than just shelling out cash for a degree.

(Psst… I'll be going into even more detail on education in the next chapter—for those who need a little more convincing that a formal degree *isn't* the path to more money!)

Connecting the Dots

I've noticed a pattern in my years of helping others earn more income. It is a *major* mistake that shatters so many people's attempts to realize their dreams. A lot of us start out seeking to solve only our *own* problems. It starts out innocent enough. "I need money so I can support my family" *sounds* like a noble cause, doesn't it? But it'll come back to bite you because making money requires you solve *other people's* problems.

So the most important truth of all that I want you to understand about money is this: *Making money is not about you.* Flip the switch on this in your mind. Instead of thinking about yourself first, focus on other people. Solve *their* problems, and your own problem (needing money!) will dissipate naturally. Even fear and self-doubt won't be such a bother anymore—instead, you'll be so focused on solving someone else's problem that you won't focus on the fear.

Solve other people's problems, and you'll make money. *That's* the truth.

CHAPTER SEVEN
The Truth About Education

I t's more than just myths about money that keep people from writing their own income stories. I touched on it briefly in the last chapter, and we'll hit it hard here… it's myths about *education*.

Education-related myths cause people to depend on exorbitantly expensive formal institutions whenever they want to learn anything new. People take out unnecessary student loans to finance that "education." Unsuspecting individuals spend several years on a whole bunch of irrelevant prerequisites before they're even allowed to start learning in their desired subject. Instead of enabling more people to succeed, many higher education institutions *keep people* from succeeding.

I'll expose these myths in this chapter. As you read through them, ask yourself whether these myths hold you back. If they are, commit to reprogramming your brain like you did with the money myths. Take out that trash!

Education Myth No. 1: College Creates Income.

An entire generation of young adults believes they need a degree to get a good job. They think they're destined to struggle without one. We're *inundated* with stats about the *value* of college degrees. We're told college graduates earn $1 million more than high school graduates over the course of an average lifetime. We're told college graduates have better job security, jobs with benefits, and more. Parents get shamed into starting a college savings plan for kids they haven't even *conceived* yet. If high school students even *suggest* skipping college, all hell can break loose!

The stats about college graduates earning more might be accurate when spread across millions of people... but they're irrelevant to any individual person. Because here's a fact higher education doesn't want you to know: College doesn't create income. *You do.*

Too many people who have no college degree let that hold them back. Some spend their entire life thinking they'll never make good money without a degree. Others quit their jobs to go back to college because they don't know what else to do to earn more money. Once they get that degree—the one they believed would solve their problem—they find they're *still* dependent on someone else to give them a job. Maybe the economy's bad or the college oversold how in-demand their program was... and there aren't any jobs available locally. No matter the case, they barely earn enough money to pay their minimum student loan payment.

College *used* to help you stand out. Now, almost *everyone* has a college degree, and a Master of Business Administration (MBA) was the ticket to a great job. So thousands of people flocked to business school, took out even more loans, and got a prized MBA. Now, it seems like *everyone* has an MBA. When nearly every college in the country begins selling (yes; colleges sell!) what used to be scarce, the value goes down over time—sometimes very quickly. (Ask me about the time I spent $50 on a "rare" Beanie Baby at the flea market when I was 11, and I'll tell you a similar story.) Nowadays an MBA isn't as special anymore because anyone can get one just about anywhere—even online!

A regular ol' bachelor's degree like mine is about as meaningful in today's job economy as a high school diploma was in the sixties. They're a dime a dozen. It might get you an interview with someone who went to the same school but that's about it. You'll spend four precious years of your life in college, and for what? The privilege of fighting tooth and nail with your entire graduating class for entry-level jobs? Sounds like fun... not!

If you want to make money without having to work for "the man," forget about your degree. Focus on building an arsenal of in-demand skills to create income for yourself. For me and many of my students, that started with proofreading—and our skills grew from there.

I built courses and other sources of income. Everything I do helps people quit their commutes, invest in themselves, and earn income. Many of my students realized how simple it was for them to learn one skill. Just *one* skill is all they needed to start earning income, and they knew they didn't need college to learn that skill.

The same goes for you. All it takes is for you to master *one* skill to start earning income. What happens after that might surprise you. For me and many of my students—especially when we reaped the rewards of that first skill—it inspired us to learn even more. We thought, "Why stop here?" We'd proven to ourselves the power of mastering just one skill, and the gears started turning. Mo' skills; mo' money. We could learn more to earn more... so we did.

I didn't become the owner of a multimillion-dollar media company at 30 years old by selling extra bread. I certainly didn't get where I am now because of my bachelor's degree. Not a single person asked to see my diploma before sending me proofreading work. Not a single person asked to see it before they enrolled in my online courses, either.

Before someone will give you any of their hard-earned cash, they need to trust you. A piece of paper doesn't guarantee you can trust someone anymore. I heard a joke once that made me laugh but also scared me a little: What do you call a doctor who barely passed his exams? *Doctor.* See my point? You can't know someone is really good at what they do just because they passed college. It takes more than that to gain the trust of a paying client.

When I started, I had limited skills and my rates reflected that. As I developed my skills and added new ones, my rates—and income—rose as well. I didn't go back to college; I just added skills. I streamlined my processes so I could be as efficient and effective as possible, and I learned how to market myself. Three years and a lot of mistakes later, I was a millionaire. Because of that, when someone asks me if my degree has helped me, my honest-to-God answer is no. It didn't teach me *anything* I needed to know to do what I'm doing today. In fact, everything I'm doing to run my business today I learned *after* I graduated with my bachelor's degree. I got my first entry-level job three months before I graduated, so I didn't even get my first job because of my degree.

Learning changed everything for me, and it can for you too. The whole point of this book is to inspire you to learn more stuff so you can earn more money. Get excited about what your life could look like if you put new knowledge into your brain and then *use* that knowledge to solve problems. Big problems or small problems; it doesn't matter—as long as you know solving problems is what will increase your income.

So what could your life look like in a year? Five years? Ten years? As for me, I have no idea what life will be like a decade from now, but it'll probably blow me away. As long as I keep learning, I'll keep earning—I just won't be going back to college for the learning part!

Education Myth No. 2: Your Degree is Your Future.

Our society has tricked us into believing we need to go to college to build a career we love. We need to choose a degree program. We need to "learn stuff" for four to six years. Then *BOOM!* a fantastic job in our field will fall in our lap and pay us six figures to start—in the location of our dreams, too! That's a lie.

The truth is, many people's degrees quickly become irrelevant. The rare exceptions to the rules are for careers like doctors and lawyers. Those *require* degrees, and they also require continuing education to stay relevant. In my case, four years of college got me a $12-per-hour desk job. *Holla!*

Somehow a bunch of us think we shouldn't have to learn anything new after college. I was that way. I thought my degree entitled me to a high-paying job. I had a friend who got an MBA and was sorely disappointed to learn she *still* didn't qualify for her dream job.

Some folks think they're not capable of learning anything new. Once they decide on their degree, that's the path they've chosen—no pivoting allowed! Instead of pivoting or adding new skills when they discover their path isn't all it's cracked up to be, they sit atop a mountain of debt, wasted time, and poor-paying jobs... and complain.

But wait! There's more.

Most people think that knowledge is power. Nope! It's not enough, not anymore. In the days before the internet, if you didn't know something, it would take *a long freakin' time* to figure it out. Today, you don't really need to *know* anything; an answer is just a Google search, "Alexa!" or "Hey, Siri," away. Thank goodness I don't need to remember the names of every single Zac Efron movie or how to get to my mom's house—there's an app for that!

Real power comes not from knowing stuff; it comes from *doing* stuff with what you know. There's power in the sheer admission that you don't know everything—and that if you learn something new, you can *do* something new. If you do something new, then you'll get something new... which could be mo' money than you ever thought you'd see in your lifetime!

My degree did not teach me how to proofread. It did not teach me how to build a website. It did not teach me how to write books like this one. It did not teach me how to market myself or find clients. It did not teach me how to use social media. College didn't teach me how to *do* anything, but I didn't let that stop me from learning and seeking help when I needed it. Although I hesitated at first—old beliefs die hard!—I learned the skills I needed to build my business *without* the hassle (and expense) of college.

If I wasn't on scholarship, my degree would have cost tens of thousands of dollars. Tuition alone was $30,000, and that didn't include books or supplies. I'd have been pretty ticked off if I had actually paid that much for the degree I got. I'd have been even more ticked off if I had taken out student loans to fund it. Half the stuff I learned was the *same* stuff I learned in high school. And... spoiler alert! I've *still* never used about 85% of it. I could have learned the other 15% the same way I learned the skills I used to build my business. (Hey, if you want to know the entire history of human taxonomy, let me know! No? How about how to solve a quadratic polynomial? Still no? Geez... tough crowd!)

Moral of the story? Don't let your college degree—or its irrelevance, or your lack of one altogether—keep you from building your dream life. Don't let the $200,000 you spent on a degree keep you from building a life you love. I know past mistakes can sting a *lot*, but it's never too late to start over. You don't have to waste the rest of your life being broke or miserable because of a decision you made at 17 years old. Not everyone will need to make as dramatic a shift as I did. Sometimes you hate your job, and a different job does the trick. But way too many people stay at a job or in a career they hate because they "invested" so much time and money in their degree. Which would you rather waste? The money you spent on a degree... or the remaining years of your life?

There's nothing you can do right now to go back in time and not get that degree or your student loan debt. But there *is* something you can do about your future. In fact, you're on that path right now just by reading this book.

College doesn't teach you everything you need to know. It's not a weakness to admit it. It's also not a weakness to admit that you didn't have all the answers at 17 years old.

Put it this way: Would you let the next 17-year-old you meet decide what you're going to do for work for the rest of your life? Of course not.

How about this? You walk up to two 17-year-olds standing next to each other in the mall. You wait patiently for them to stop texting each other. Whoever looks up first gets to choose your career. Sounds ridiculous, right?

So why do so many adults (or big kids like me) feel trapped by decisions their 17-year-old selves made?

Don't give up because you thought a "communications" degree seemed cool when you were 17. Don't stay miserable because the teen version of you decided to follow her boyfriend to art school. Would you walk into the nearest high school and hire the head of the drama club to be your life coach? That's essentially what you're doing if you let your high school self control your future.

Don't worry about what the 17-year-old version of you thought was *cool*, either. Seventeen-year-old me didn't leave the house without makeup, but she watched *Spongebob*. I've come a long way. You're as cool as you've ever been *right now*, so start where you are. Starting today, you can turn the *rest* of your life into the *best* of your life!

Education Myth No. 3: You Can't Teach an Old Dog New Tricks.

I know what you're thinking: *"It's too late for me!"* Even after the last section where I mentioned it is never too late to start over, you might be thinking you're the exception. Le sigh. Too many people lose hope way too soon because they feel like an *old dog*. They think their ship has sailed. Every opportunity has passed them by already because they're 10, 20, or even 40 years out of college or "past their prime."

The exact opposite is true. In fact, the further away from college you are, *the less your degree matters*. That's great news! On top of that, the world is changing so fast that some people's degrees are irrelevant almost the day they graduate. This year's technology will be obsolete by the same time next year. There's gobs of stuff I've learned in just the last three years that's already outdated today.

The truth is, you learn new things all the time. You might not think of it as learning, but it is. With a traditional job, your *company* might not want to teach you new tricks, but *you* can teach *yourself* new tricks. Yet too many people don't see that possibility and sell themselves way too short. They don't connect the dots between skills and income. Some folks are intimidated by technology or online learning methods, so they default to what's familiar: going to college and getting stranded on another mountain of debt. Don't fall into *that* trap!

Following the "familiar" can fool you into living a mediocre life. In some cases, defaulting to the familiar could be exactly why you're dissatisfied with your life and/or your income now. You were just doing what you were told, after all; you were just following in your parents' footsteps. Whatever the familiar is for you, know that *there is more*. There is *more* for you, and you can have it.

"Old dogs" *can* learn new tricks. The "trick" is not to try to teach them a million tricks at once. *Anyone* can learn and apply skills to make income from anywhere. The possibilities are endless—I'm here to help you weed through them all to find what works for you.

3 Truths About Education

We've been programmed to think our degree *creates* income, our degree is our future, and you can't teach an old dog new tricks. Those are *lies*.

A degree doesn't create income; you do. If you have a day job, your degree doesn't get a paycheck; you do. If you stop showing up, eventually your paycheck is going to stop showing up, too. If you don't have a degree, that's not a good reason to give up; it's a perfect reason to get started! The economy and technology are both changing so rapidly that it is now easier than ever to learn skills and earn money.

Your degree might be your present; it might be your past, but it doesn't have to determine your future unless you let it. You wouldn't let a 17-year-old mall rat choose your next career path, would you? So don't let your 17-year-old self's decision about college determine what you do for the rest of your life. Make different choices, and you'll get different results. It's that simple.

And you most definitely *can* teach an old dog new tricks. It's never too late! No matter your age or how many years have passed since you got out of school or even how fast technology changes, the basic principle behind how to make money will always be the same: To earn money, you need to use a skill to solve a problem for someone else.

That's the truth.

CHAPTER EIGHT
The Truth About Work

Y ou might have noticed many of the myths we've busted so far are related. Our beliefs about money are often a *result* of our beliefs about education, work, business, and success. Up next are myths about work.

What "work" means has evolved a lot over the last few decades. What was once considered way too risky for the average bear has become the norm for many. Yet there's still a lot of skepticism based on old information—and misinformation—and that skepticism is what keeps otherwise very capable people in dead-end jobs with limited income.

You're better than that, and you know it! So the same goes for these myths as the last ones. As you read through them, ask yourself whether you believe any of them. Are they holding you back? If they are, commit to reprogramming your brain to believe the truth: You have the power to work exactly the way you want!

Work Myth No. 1: Traditional Jobs are More Secure Than Freelance Work.

A lot of people assume that freelance work is *riskier* than traditional jobs. You get a *reliable* paycheck every week or two with traditional jobs. You don't have to rely on new clients or customers to pay you or chase invoices from people who don't pay.

They like the "guarantee" of having a few grand added to their bank accounts every two weeks. They think it's too much of a "risk" to be the sole person responsible for their own income. They think the "risk" of working at home isn't worth it.

Those people are wrong.

They're either looking at it wrong... or they're *doing it* wrong. When done right, work-at-home jobs are *less* risky than traditional jobs. They're *more* secure, too.

It's true you don't have to find new clients or customers to make basic money in a traditional job. But—big but—do you really want to limit yourself to *basic* money? Having a basic job means you'll only earn basic income... and basic income, especially when someone else is in charge of giving it to you, *is way riskier.*

Let's unpack that a bit. With a traditional job, you rely on one company—and sometimes one unreasonable boss—for 100% of your income. You could get on their bad side by ordering cheese that "isn't artisanal enough." Worse, you could get all your work done by lunchtime and face a choice like I did. You could either spend the rest of a perfectly good day chained to a desk doing other people's work... or you could do what you want with your time. If you do what you want in the traditional job environment, you risk getting fired and losing *all* your income. You could even get bullied into paying your boss $2,000 on the way out, like I was.

My story isn't unique. Once I started sharing it, it blew me away how many people chimed in to tell me that they, too, suddenly saw their income disappear with little warning. Debbie Gartner found herself in a similar situation. Debbie's now a full-time virtual assistant and blogger at TheFlooringGirl.com, but she once relied on traditional work—she thought she was safe… until she wasn't.

Here's how Debbie describes what happened to her.

> **❝** I found myself in a very scary situation with a **huge** amount of debt, huge mortgage, and no job—and only 24 hours' notice. I had no time to lose due to my huge mortgage and cost of living.
>
> I decided to work on monetizing my blog while doing freelancing at the same time. Monetizing a blog takes time, but I needed instant income. Since I already knew how to blog, that's what I now do for my clients. I've been freelancing around 12 hours per week and earn around $4,000 a month from that.

You can see the same formula at work with Debbie. She had a skill. In her case, that skill was blogging. So she marketed herself as a blogger for hire and, working just 12 hours per week, she earns $4,000 per month from home!

Debbie's the perfect example of using skills you already have to make a full-time living from home ASAP. Now she has multiple clients, so even if one or two drop her, she still has enough income to cover her bills and expenses. The best part? She has the skills and know-how to find additional clients—additional income—*whenever she wants.*

Real "job security" isn't in a j-o-b anymore, my friend. It's in your *skills.*

Work Myth No. 2: You Need to Work More to Make More.

Although it took me a while, after I got fired I realized if I wanted to earn more money, I had to *choose* to learn more skills. I stopped believing that my degree, my boss, and my location were the reasons I couldn't do more with my life.

Looking back, I see how I've always rebelled against this particular myth. It started with winning the bread-selling competition, then by refusing to just sit and wait for the phone to ring at the animal hospital. In my final job, I stopped doing other people's work when I finished mine early.

I stopped letting myself think I needed a different degree, boss, or location to make more. I stopped looking at money as something people give you in exchange for your time. And I stopped thinking work had to be a drag or something I would work to "retire" from when I got older (more on that in a minute). I now know you do *not* have to work more to earn more.

This mindset shift certainly didn't happen overnight. Not even close. Sometimes I still struggle with the idea that I should be spending more hours of my day cranking out magic for my tribe. I'd do that if I *really* cared about them, right?! I still feel an invisible expectation that if I'm not at my desk for eight hours a day, then I'm not doing enough work. I even feel like a fraud sometimes. These feelings are part of *every* entrepreneur's journey, though—and it's part of my job to help you deal with them!

My journey is still in its beginning stages too. I'm not done yet. In fact, I'll probably look back at this book in five years and laugh. But that's the way it goes—we're always growing and learning. If you ever expect to be "done," you're dead. Our society conditions us to work, work, work and save, save, save so we can be "done" with work when we're older. We'll have time to do what we want when we *retire.*

The race to retirement assumes we don't enjoy what we do enough to do it all the time. It also assumes we'll actually *make it* to retirement age. We're not guaranteed tomorrow, much less the next year or decade, so where is the sense in denying ourselves enjoyment until we reach a certain age? There is no sense in it. Life is too short to wait and enjoy it later. There's another way. You can enjoy your work *now*, make money, *and* do a crap ton of stuff you want to do.

Bad things happen when we retire our noggins. Both my grandparents on my mom's side had Alzheimer's Disease, so I'm keen to keep my brain jogging along for many years to come. The best way to jog your brain, in my opinion, is to keep solving problems. If you always focus energy on solving the world's problems, you'll never have to worry about where money will come from—and your brain will love it.

That's key, too: Using our brains feels good! If I spend even a few days on the couch watching Netflix, drinking alcohol, lounging by the pool—or otherwise not using my brain—I feel yucky. My first day back to solving problems usually starts out rough, but once I get going, I can't deny that I feel better when I'm using my brain again. It's very similar to exercise… hard to start, but we always feel better after a good, sweaty workout! Solving problems is exercise for the brain, and the side effect is more money.

Blame Henry Ford for inventing the eight-hour work day (but thanks for the cars, bro). Lots of studies show that humans *can't* be productive for eight hours a day. Problem solving doesn't *require* you to sit at your desk for the best hours of every day. It depends on the work, of course, and some people totally dig office work where they can zone out and get paid. Whatever floats your boat. Point is, if you can solve someone's problem in four hours, there is no need to sit there idly for an additional four hours.

In most cases, clients only care about the end product. Did you do what you promised? They want the value they paid for. If you tell them you're going to proofread a transcript and you do it well, they're happy. They don't care if you did it from the beach or in an office down the street.

Work Myth No. 3: You Don't Have What it Takes to Run a Business.

When I was 23, I posted a status on my Facebook profile that said, simply, "a higher IQ would be nice…" That's all I posted. Seven years later, it popped up as a Facebook memory, and it hit me hard.

If you want to share in my agony, I put a screenshot of the post on the Resources page. You can see it at WorkAtHomeSchool.com/BookResources.

I changed a lot in the seven years following my post. It was a heck of a process... a real metamorphosis. I went from a college grad with a useless degree... to a $12-per-hour desk job... to fired... to a struggling freelancer... to making $40,000 per year as a proofreader... to a blogger... to an entrepreneur... to a self-made millionaire—all in seven years.

But when I was 23, I thought I needed to be smarter. When things weren't going my way in the moment, I made excuses. When I wasn't making the money I wanted, it was "because of my degree" or "because my boss was stingy" or "because of where I lived."

"If I had a better degree" or "a more generous boss" or "if I lived in New York City," I said, "things would be better. I would be successful." Yet here I am, years later, still living in the Central Florida area. I have the same degree, but that's about it. No more boss. No more commute. No more measly paycheck. And I built my dream house.

I didn't work *more*. I didn't get *smarter*. I just learned more skills and then marketed them to the right people. I got different information and took different action. I realized that *I* was the problem and that I'd used my less-than-genius intellect as an excuse to live a mediocre life!

Taking different action meant that I invested my time differently. Instead of sitting on the couch watching Grey's Anatomy all day, I used a chunk of that time to write blog articles, practice my tech skills, and learn all I could about online marketing. Most days, I made progress. Other days I screwed up and took a few steps backward. Then there were the days I spun around in circles, making no progress at all. But even after a bad day, waking up the next day and doing *something* to move forward helped me pick myself up, dust myself off, and get back on track. It's not how quickly you move that matters; it's how *consistently* you move—especially on days when you don't feel like it!

That's how creating your own freedom works. It's progressive. It doesn't happen overnight. It's not like you wake up one day and say, "I'm going to transform today!" and then *BOOM!* you're a new person. It's your everyday choices that create the transformation over time. Even the smallest ones matter. I didn't need a higher IQ; I just needed to keep learning and implementing what I'd learned.

Sometimes it takes lots of time, and more often than not you don't even realize you've transformed. It's like watching grass grow. You never see it happening, but then one day it's standing so tall and proud that you can't find the front door. Okay; so it's not *exactly* like watching grass grow, but I think you know what I mean. *Become the grass.* (More on that concept in the 28-day launch plan!)

You catch a glimpse of the person you were and see the true power of your choices. That's what happened when my Facebook memory popped up in my feed that morning. It hit me like a ton of bricks. I hadn't felt the transformation happening, but it happened. Bill Gates once said, "Most people overestimate what they can do in one year and underestimate what they can do in ten years." I think that's largely true, but what I've noticed over the years is that many people also underestimate what's possible to accomplish in a year—

they believe it will take too long to reap the rewards of action they take, so they never get started.

That's one reason I started the Work-At-Home Heroes podcast. Almost all of my guests since I launched it in January 2017 are real people who've been working from home for between six months and two years. Their tales of transformation will make your jaw drop! I wanted to spread their stories far and wide to prove that learning and taking action can dramatically transform your life—if you give it a chance.

Remember how I gave myself six months with my first blog? Many bloggers need more time than I did to see a return on their blog, and I hate to think that if things had gone differently for me that I would've given up after only six months. Giving up after only six months seems *insane* to me now. In the grand scheme of things, six months is nothing, but it can also be everything.

Start. Then do *not* give up, even if it's been more than six months; even if it's been more than a year. Because the thing is, the time will pass anyway… it might even stop for us all together without notice. We can't know exactly when our time is up, so we might as well invest our time wisely and *do the thing. Try* to create the life of your dreams… and see what happens. Let's not get to the end of our lives and wonder where the time went—where *life* went—and why we didn't make better use of it when we had the chance.

We must choose wisely. Every day matters. Choosing to get out of bed a little earlier to work on your course matters. Choosing to be kind to someone who's been disrespectful to you matters. How we spend every second is a choice… and all those choices add up.

It's like investing regularly into a 401(k) at work. Over time, those small deposits compound with interest—and it adds up. Similarly, the choices you make every day will compound over time. A bunch of small choices grow into big rewards. I like to think of every choice I make as a potential investment in Future Me. Every time you do something scary or hard or when you don't feel like it, you're making an investment in Future You. Sometimes positive choices in the "now" give you a return the same day! If I wake up groggy or not feeling like doing anything, but I decide to jump on my trampoline for 20 minutes anyway, *Future Me* will feel better and have more energy that same day. Even if Present Me doesn't feel like it, I make the choice for Future Me.

You might have bad days, too. You might make some choices that lead to not-so-good results. I *still* do. But over time—in my case, I'm talking about seven years—positive choices and actions will lead to positive results. If your entire life's journey were a mutual fund chart, your positive choices every day would flow up and to the right! It won't be a straight line; it'll be a zigzag up and down, just like a mutual fund chart. But it will trend up. The key is not to give up when the line zags down for a little while. The only way to see the upward trend is to wait it out. The only way to fail is to give up… and *giving up is a choice.*

So I want to encourage you—especially if you're new to the work-from-anywhere world. Forget about the short term. Consider each choice for what it can do for the long term. For Future You. Sometimes you won't want to get out of bed to proofread that transcript. Sometimes you won't want to write that blog post or answer your email. Sometimes you'll dread calling a client. And sometimes you won't want to attend a webinar or take a course to refine your skills. I get it. I had a lot of those days.

But every time you do, it brings you closer to your goal. You won't make money by *not* taking action. All the choices you make today impact who you become tomorrow. You don't need another degree. You don't need a higher IQ. You don't need some complicated business model or a big business loan. All you need to make money is a skill you can use to solve a problem. Big or small. *Anyone* reading this can solve *some* kind of problem for someone else.

It's all a choice. What will you choose?

3 Truths About Work

These lies about work keep people in insecure jobs that pay them for their time and limit their income. You'll never reach your potential without understanding these three work truths.

Most traditional jobs are *less secure* than writing your own income story. That's because the decision of *one* person can take your income straight to zero. I don't care how much your health insurance costs at work. I don't care how many fringe benefits they give you. Those are all things you can purchase on your own. In fact, they're things you can often buy *cheaper* on your own. Like it or not, too, the "benefits" you get at a traditional job still come at a cost: your freedom.

You don't need to work more to make more. You just need to make a different choice. *It's all a choice.* Choose to develop or refine a skill that solves a problem. The bigger the problem, the more you can earn by solving it. Choose to market that skill. Choose to add value. Choose to charge what you're worth. People who make the most money charge for the value they provide, not the time it took to provide it. I can help you with all those things, but I can't make choices for you. Only you possess that power.

Finally, anyone reading this book can start writing their own income story. You *do* have what it takes. Say it to yourself again right now: *"I write my own income story."* At this point, you've read my words about choice, taking action, and never giving up over and over again. I've heard that the average person needs to hear something 19 times before they'll believe it enough to take action. While I'm not keeping count on how many times I've told you the same things over and over so far, I know someone out there needs the repetition. I know this because at one point not long ago, *I needed it.* I needed someone to tell me—more than just once—that my success was up to me. That my choices were my power.

I'll give you the exact steps to get started. It's up to you to take those steps. You don't need another degree, and you don't need to be a genius. You need to choose, and you need to *act.* It'll be scary at times, but you won't be alone unless you choose to be. Again... *it's all a choice.*

That's the truth.

CHAPTER NINE
The Truth About Business and Success

We've got one more set of myths to bust. *More myths?!* *Yeah; I know what you're thinking. Get to the good part already, Caitlin! Tell me HOW to do this!*

I'm getting there; I promise. Knowing how is actually the easy part of starting a business. So many people know exactly what their first step is, but they never take it. Why not? Because they're caught in a web of lies—they believe the very same myths we've been debunking for the last few chapters. That's why I'm spending so much time breaking these down. You *must* make sure you're free from the web or it *will* trip you up. Speaking from experience.

Onward! These three myths about business and success are so far from the truth, it's hard to know where they originated. Let's dig in!

Business and Success Myth No. 1: Other People's Success Means There's No Room for Your Success.

One of the most difficult lies to get over is that other people's success indicates there's less opportunity for you to succeed as well. Some people think other people's success means you've done something wrong. Others think it's too late for them if others have succeeded in their area—as if the lake were only so big and all the fish are gone. If you believe that, I've got news for you: The world isn't a lake, and money isn't fish!

Way too many people give up on their dream after seeing other people already doing what they want to do. It usually starts when you get excited about a skill you can market and you type it into Google. When you discover that 3, 4, or 54 people are already selling the same skills—or *big* companies already selling the exact same skills—you think it's too late. I see this all the time at Proofread Anywhere. "Oh, no! The market's already *saturated!* There's probably not any work left for me." That kind of mindset makes me want to punch a puppy. Or barf. Or both.

Because it's just not true. In fact, the opposite is true! It's a *good thing* if other people are already doing what you want to do. First, if you see other people offering the same service you offer, it indicates there's a *market* for that service. It shows that the service is in demand, which is exactly what you want. It means you won't have to convince people to pay you for your services because people are already *accustomed* to paying for those services. Trust me when I tell you, it's much easier to sell a service that people are used to paying for than to sell something *nobody's* offering. There's plenty of work to go around—especially if you're willing to go find it.

When I got started proofreading, I was far from the only person doing it. There were already *thousands* of people making money proofreading. I still freelanced my way to a full-time income. Then I blogged my way to a brand-new career as chief blogger and teacher at Proofread Anywhere, where I helped *thousands more* people make money proofreading. Occasionally, prospective students ask me why I chose to share my knowledge instead of keeping all the clients to myself. *"Aren't you saturating the market by training new proofreaders?"* they'd ask. There is *no way* I could proofread everything myself, for one thing. There is far more text to proofread than I can handle alone—and there's more and more every day.

We further box ourselves in by thinking we can only work with people who live in our hometowns. We even convince ourselves that something doesn't exist simply because we've never heard of it. It's like we live *in* a box sometimes, isn't it? So many possibilities; so many opportunities exist outside the box, under the box... heck; there are probably opportunities *in* the box itself, but you can't see them because why? *It's dark in there!*

Believing there is a limited amount of opportunity in the world is akin to believing there is a limited amount of money. It's just not true. Money is unlimited, and so is opportunity. Besides time, the only real limits when it comes to earning money are the ones you place on yourself. It's the box we live in. So get out of the box. Better... *destroy* the box. Use it to light a fire. Under your butt.

A second reason competition in the marketplace is a good thing is because you can meet all kinds of people to learn from. Warren Buffett once famously said, "It's good to learn from your mistakes. It's better to learn from other people's mistakes." I love that quote almost as much as I love my dog, Buffett, whom I named after good ol' Warren. When other people are doing what you want to do, you get to learn from their mistakes. In fact, that's one of the most valuable parts of Work-At-Home School. Students get to learn from all of our instructors' mistakes, saving them valuable time and lots of headaches.

When you find other people doing what you want to do, you get to learn from them. How much do they charge? What services do they offer? How do they advertise? What do the ones that charge the highest prices do differently from the ones who charge lower prices? This information can help you a lot when determining how you want to run things for yourself. (You'll be doing a bit of this research yourself inside the 28-day launch plan at the end of the book!)

Finally, newbies often have significant *advantages* over established businesses. They might not have the same budget or contacts, but they're quicker and have far less overhead. They can afford to take small risks because they don't have to worry about paying rent or employee salaries. They can make decisions faster than big businesses. As someone who regularly hires all kinds of virtual help, I much prefer working with freelancers over big "do it all" agencies. The service is much more personal.

So to recap, if someone's already doing what you want to do, it's *proof* that you're onto something. It's an opportunity to learn and a chance to set yourself apart with a level of personalized service and attention only *you* can provide!

Business and Success Myth No. 2: Successful People Don't Fail.

It's easy to think the most successful people are the ones who never fail. You hardly ever see anyone share their failures on Facebook; do you? Very few souls are brave enough to talk about the times they got cocktail sauce all over themselves at a networking event or sent out an email with a big, fat typo in it (which is *especially* brutal if you're me). Nope. Instead, you see a lot of staged vacation pics and business celebrations that incite envy. If you evaluate your own potential for success only by what you see in your Facebook newsfeed, it's easy to believe these people have it all and that there's nary a rough patch in sight.

Social media can be demoralizing if you're struggling. It happens to everyone. Think back to the last time you saw a celebratory Facebook post from someone. Allow me to channel my inner psychologist for a moment. How do those posts make you feel? Inspired? Or envious? What do you think of those people? Do you think they must do everything right? Do you think they got lucky? Do you think they succeeded just because they didn't fail?

Nothing is further from the truth. All you see on social media are snapshots—mere moments in time. You see the highlight reel of people's lives, not the bloopers.

I guarantee you that behind every success story you see, there are at least a dozen missteps. At *least*. This is especially true in the work-from-anywhere world. I've failed more times than I can count. The truth is, everyone who's achieved success has failed a bunch of times.

It's hard to keep your chin up when you hit those bumps in the road. It's easy to think you're not cut out for the freedom lifestyle, even if you want it badly. I promise you that's hardly ever the case. Successful people fail. The difference is they don't give up when it happens. They keep going and adopt the mindset that failure is just a hurdle to hop over. It's not a reason to turn around and go home; it's part of the journey, and you always *learn* from it.

I like to say there's no such thing as failure—there's only learning. As much as it stinks to have a project or an idea not pan out, there is always something to learn from the experience. Take it from me: In the first year after I started my blog, I attempted to start an additional *three* online businesses. I ended up shutting down all three. *I failed.* No biggie. I just applied what I'd learned to something that was a better fit for me.

You'll find your fit, too. That's what I'm here to help you do. But I want you to make a promise—not to me but to yourself. Even when it's hard... even when you don't feel like it... even when someone hiding behind a computer screen calls you names, *don't give up.* Keep pushing through when you think you've failed. Master your skill and market it. Be relentless in your pursuit of the life you've dreamed of. You can make it real.

The Most Expensive Typo in History

In 1962, NASA launched the Mariner I rocket only to see it explode less than five minutes after liftoff. The cause? A missing hyphen in the mathematical code. YIKES! (Too bad they didn't have a world-class proofreader looking out for missing hyphens...)

Guess how much that missing hyphen cost the government? A cool $80 million—or about $650 million adjusted for inflation as of 2017. Talk about a catastrophic error!

Even the smartest, most qualified people in the world make mistakes. The good news is your screw-ups likely won't cost $650 million. But—big but!—if you let it scare you from pushing forward, it can cost you something much greater than that. It can cost you your dream business. It can cost you your dream lifestyle. It can cost you your dream *life.*

What if everyone was too scared to try something new because they were afraid of making a mistake?

Take starting a new business, for example. That's a scary thing to do. If it weren't, everyone would be doing it. Fortunately, starting a business usually doesn't involve the kind of math that could blow up a rocket. *Whew.*

But it's still scary. Heck... my beloved Proofread Anywhere almost never came to be. I almost let my fear of failure and inadequacy stop me. I convinced myself nobody wanted to learn from me. I was wrong and my fear was wrong, but it was, as they say, "the fear I held near." Most of the time the "fear we hold near" is a) imaginary, b) unwarranted, c) not *that* bad, or d) all of the above.

Successful people keep going even when they're scared or after they failed. So give yourself some grace. It can be hard to learn new skills, start a new business, and work for your first freelance clients. You can't expect to be perfect, and you don't *have* to be perfect. Everyone makes mistakes—even the most brilliant mathematicians on Earth! Just try not to blow up any rockets.

Not to be cocky, but it's fair to say I'd qualify as a success under most people's definition, right? I became a millionaire at 30 years old. I did it by helping a bunch of people break free from overbearing bosses, ditch their soul-crushing commutes, and dwarf their minuscule paychecks from the comfort of their own homes. And you already know about *some* of my failures getting to that point, like in 2011 when I got fired from my job. #fail

You also know I spent over $7,000 on personal training school only to quickly realize it was a mistake. I had been thinking I would start a mobile personal training business. I ended up teaching a bunch of classes at a gym with another miserable commute. #fail

Remember those three businesses I tried to start the first year I had my blog? The truth is, I spent *most of 2015* failing. Like, over and over again. Ready for this? My cheeks are beet red as I write, but here it goes...

First, I spent six months and a *lot* of money trying to build a directory website in the court reporting niche. I failed miserably because, while I love teaching people to proofread transcripts for court reporters, I had no passion for court reporting itself. I let the project die. #expensivefail

Second, I built an online course on how to create an online course. Eight people paid $1,000 for me to teach them for six months. I invested a lot of time building that and helped those eight people get started. It was fun while it lasted, but I soon learned that I didn't want to teach people how to create online courses. I eventually shut that project down too. #anotherexpensivefail

Finally, I built an entire e-commerce store to sell T-shirts with proofreading-related quips on them. I thought they were cool. Heck; they *were* cool... but it was a bad fit for me. I eventually shut that down, too—having sold a paltry three T-shirts—because... wait for it... I didn't want to sell T-shirts. #somuchfail

The hits didn't stop in 2015, either. In 2017, I was forced to cancel a live event I had planned for more than a year because not enough people could make it. #painfulfail

I'd list *even more* of my failures here, but frankly it would take up way too much space. The truth is, no matter where you are in your journey, you're going to try some stuff that won't work for you. It happens to *everyone*. If you're anything like me, you've tried quite a few things in the past that didn't pan out and, like me, you may have called them "failures."

So I'll say it again: There is no such thing as failure; there is only learning. Learning about yourself, what you like, and what you're good at is important. Learning what you *don't* like is just as valuable as learning what you do like, and often it's in figuring out the "don't likes" that we discover our true calling. Every time I've failed, I've learned something. Even when I feel a twinge of regret about one of those stepping stones, I focus in on what I learned about myself in the process. There's always gold in the ashes.

Business and Success Myth No. 3: Working at Home is EASY!

A lot of the so-called experts out there want you to believe that working from anywhere is all about beaches and "printing money." They sell the dream without sharing the reality—all in an effort to get you to buy some obscure, poorly written eBook that reveals the "secret" idea that will make you a millionaire overnight. *So not cool.*

Very few so-called experts are brave enough to share how much actual *work* is involved in building a business from home. Why? I think it's because they're afraid of scaring people away and losing sales on their weird eBooks. My thoughts on that… scaring people away is *good*. If someone's scared off by the fact that working from home takes actual work, they're not going to get along very well with me! Work is my favorite four-letter word.

I want to share as much truth as possible—all the good *and* the bad—because you're going to experience both. That's the reality.

Working from home is hard. Sometimes you'll work long hours, especially in the beginning. You might struggle to find the right place to start. A lot of people start businesses only to realize they hate them, like I did in 2015. I did a *ton* of work by myself at first too—that was before I learned how to delegate to virtual assistants! I remember working 14- or 16-hour days while living in Santiago, Chile, in a 400-square-foot apartment with no air conditioning. I drank an entire bottle of white wine almost daily. Of course I'm not saying that'll be what happens to you—because you'll learn from my mistakes!—but those were really hard days. And even though I'd do things differently if I had to start over, I still don't regret those days. *All* of my mistakes have turned into lessons… most of them are in this book!

From time to time, you'll lose your inspiration. Those are the times you show up anyway. Successful people all have one thing in common, no matter their industry: They always show up. Something I've learned in disciplining my own stubborn self to show up consistently is that it's *always* worth it. I always feel better when I do the thing I don't want to do but know I should do.

You may also struggle to balance a business with your personal life or a day job, if you have one. A lot of newbies believe they have to keep their personal lives completely separate from their business.

Usually that's all in the name of professionalism. They adopt a perfectly polished, sterile persona in their business and work hard to maintain it for their customers. They pretend everything's fine while things are crumbling around them.

I take a different approach. I don't pretend everything's pretty. When things go wrong, I admit it. When I screw up, I own it. When I build an entire e-commerce store and only sell three T-shirts, I make sure to include it in my book!

I blur the line between my business and my personal life *all the time.* I share raw stuff that isn't pretty or polished even a little bit. Sometimes my rough-around-the-edges personality causes grouchy people sitting at their keyboards to hurl insults and send me long emails telling me how "unprofessional" I am. *Meh.* I've got better things to do than to deal with haters (and so do you!). My goal isn't to make everyone feel good; my goal is to help people *get results.* If that's unprofessional, then so be it!

People *like* doing business with other people. Pretending you're perfect is a waste of energy. If I only shared stuffy, explanatory, how-to pieces, people would tune me out. They'd unsubscribe from my emails and unfollow me on social media. It wouldn't matter if my advice was useful because they wouldn't relate to me. I'd go crazy, too. The funny, scary, and weird stuff is all part of working at home. So let your freak flag fly, my friend!

I like to say when you work at home, sometimes you also "home at work." You have kids, pets, or "better halves." You travel. You get sick. You get hit by natural disasters. You screw things up. *Life happens.* When you work from home or anywhere else, life and work go hand-in-hand sometimes.

So how do you deal with it?

You share. You laugh about it. You cry about it. You connect with other humans to get support. The work-at-home life is sweet because you're not tied to a location, but it can get pretty lonely for the same reason. Sharing your behind-the-scenes blooper stuff can be terrifying, but I encourage you to try it. Don't just get on your Facebook and whine, though—you don't want to be a Negative Nancy or Ned. Instead, share what you're going through *and* how you're dealing with it. That's when an otherwise "downer" post can actually inspire others in your network and help you make *real* connections with them. You might be surprised how many of your friends will chime in to share their own experiences—if you're brave enough to share your own!

We can't do this alone. We need each other! Sharing your struggles with people who understand what you're going through will create a supportive community around you. That community keeps you going when the road gets tough (or weird or rage-inducing). Your community can include your clients. Clients have options. They can *easily* find the same services elsewhere… but they can't find another *you!*

That's why I blur the line between my business and personal life. The reality is, sometimes there isn't a line between them at all.

Be Warned

All this myth busting doesn't mean you should go tell a client about your recent wart removal. It doesn't mean you should livestream your next big fight with your spouse. Keep it a *little bit* professional, yo!

I'm just saying that it's okay to break the antiquated "rules" of business a bit. Be yourself. It's not only more fun; it's *easier* to build a business this way.

In fact, "Will it allow me to be myself?" is one of the most important considerations in choosing the right fit for your work-at-home business. Don't worry too much about the written or unwritten rules or copying somebody else who seems to have the "perfect" business persona. If you were exactly like other people, there'd be no reason for anyone to do business with you. An original is always worth more than a copy!

I get a lot of emails from new subscribers who describe my transparent writing style as a breath of fresh air. "I love how you're not afraid to tell it like it is!" is a common compliment we receive. And it's true… especially with my content about mindset. I'm not afraid of offending a few people if it helps the majority build a better life for themselves. *Tough love* and all that.

Working at home *isn't* always easy. I'll never sugarcoat anything—and that's a promise.

3 Truths About Business and Success

The lies we believe about business and success kill dreams and keep people in dead-end jobs. Let's recap.

First, it doesn't matter if someone's already doing what you want to do. There's no reason you can't build a sustainable income too. Someone else's success is *proof* that people will pay for the skill you want to offer.

Second, you don't need to avoid failure to succeed. In fact, if you find yourself *failing to fail,* you're probably not trying hard enough. What you're doing might be way too easy for you to grow. The most successful people fail even as their income soars. Failure is never the end unless you decide it is. Choose to see your missteps as stepping stones. Just learn, adjust, and keep moving forward— because the only *real* way to fail is to give up.

Third, working from home isn't easy. You'll struggle at times. We all do! You'll lose motivation. You'll burn yourself out. You might drink way too much wine. Surrounding yourself with positive people who are on their own journey makes growing yourself and your income so much better. It's okay to be open about your struggles. Embrace the ugly. Be who you really are and see what happens.

That's the truth.

Sound the Trumpets!

We did it! Those are the myths—the biggest, baddest ones, anyway. If you found yourself nodding through many of these, thinking to yourself, *"Oh my gosh; it's like she's in my brain!"* you're not alone. People tell me that all the time, and it's because when I write about it publicly, it's because I'm going through it myself! I *know* what you're thinking because 99% of us have believed one or more of these myths at one time or another.

Feel free to revisit these sections as often as you need to. It's okay to have "relapses." For extra support, tune in to what's happening inside the Work-At-Home Heroes Facebook group—we discuss mindset-related issues in there quite often. What I want you to remember is that all newbies deal with negative mindsets and self-doubt. As you move forward on your journey, it may seem like it gets easier to deal with over time. Here's the thing, though: *None* of this stuff ever gets easier. *You* just get better!

And with that, it's time to move on! We're about to break down exactly how to find the right work-at-home opportunity for you.

PART TWO
(continued)

Step 2:

Level Up Your Mind and Your Skills

Investing in Yourself

CHAPTER TEN
Why What Worked for Someone Else Won't Necessarily Work for You

The best piece of advice I can give you if you're looking for a place to start is to *take your time.* A close second would be to avoid *shiny object syndrome.* Too often, I see people jumping in to the first thing they lay eyes on. They get sucked into the first webinar they watch, shell out a bunch of cash, and experience major buyer's remorse when they realize they *don't* want to do the thing they signed up for. That's why I put a lot of effort into *disqualifying* people from my courses. There are warnings *everywhere* to not enroll if you don't like X; don't enroll if you don't plan to do Y.

I want you to find something *you* like. I don't care how much money your cousin makes quilting. I don't care how much your uncle makes selling used books on Amazon. And I don't care how many pies your neighbor sells on the weekends. If it works for them, that's great, but that doesn't mean you'll have the same success.

If you hate quilting, you'll fail miserably if you try to make money quilting. Sure; you can *learn* how to quilt, but if you don't like it, you won't do the work it takes to succeed. There are certain skills that come easily to people simply because they *love* doing it. Quilting is very much one of those skills! If you hate the smell of a used book store, you probably wouldn't be too keen to buy a bunch of used books... which means you probably won't make much money reselling them on Amazon. Finally, if you don't love to bake, you'll never make enough pies to pay the bills.

Too many people chase opportunities only because someone else made money doing it. They're just chasing *money* at that point—not a long-term solution—and that's a recipe for disaster. At best, you'll struggle for a while, barely scrape out an income, and feel like you're working another job. At worst, you'll close up shop having lost a lot of time and money and be back at square one.

Chasing money is never a good idea. Remember what you've learned so far about what it takes to make money: solving problems! If you want to make *big* money, you'll need to learn to solve *big* problems. Making money is *always* about solving a problem for someone else. That's why chasing the dream of endless cash—like a carrot at a horse race—is a waste of your most precious asset: time.

So don't invest time and money into something *just* because Dandy McDoodleson down the street is swimming in greenbacks. Chances are if someone appears to have gotten rich overnight, it's either just a front to pull you in... or it wasn't legal!

Don't invest time and money into something you *think* sounds interesting either. You might end up wasting thousands of dollars and lots of time only to find yourself in debt from something that's not a good fit. That's how I ended up spending $7,000 to become a personal trainer only to learn it wasn't a good fit for the life I wanted. What I should've done is shadow a handful of trainers for a few months first just to make sure it's what I wanted to do *before* I forked over seven grand!

The right fit for you should pass a four-part test. First, it must not be a *scam*. Second, it must be able to generate *predictable profits* for your time and money. Third, it must be a good fit for your *personality*. Fourth, it should somewhat align with your *passions*. This one can get a little sticky, but I'll break it down for you!

Those are the four checkpoints in the "Is this a good fit for me?" test. The first three are pretty simple. If something you try is a scam, you'll waste time and money—you could even get turned off from the work-at-home world altogether. I've seen that mindset pop up in the Work-At-Home Heroes group from time to time. Somebody gets scammed and they're so stunned by it, they've started to believe *everything* is a scam.

Once you're sure something is legit, you need to see how it will generate predictable profits. Is the skill or product in demand? If you can't answer that question, you can still try it out, but it'll be a gamble.

If it doesn't fit your personality, you'll simply build another job you hate. For example, I am largely introverted, and it drains me to talk to people constantly. That's probably a big reason teaching fitness classes and working as a personal trainer wasn't a good fit for me.

And then there's that "sticky" one. Finding your "passion" trips so many people up! I've seen it time and time again. People waste a ton of time researching, hemming and hawing over the infinite things they could do… but then they never actually *do* anything because they're not sure they're *passionate* about it. What those folks don't realize is that sometimes you don't even *know* you're passionate about something because you've never tried it. I had no idea I'd be passionate about writing, blogging, and helping people write their own income story.

Passion can come later. If you zero in on something legit, something that's in-demand, and something you at least *like*, then that is an excellent place to start. Remember how I said that figuring out what you *don't* want to do is just as valuable as figuring out what you *do* want to do? We often figure out what we love by process of elimination. I can't say I was ever "passionate" about proofreading! Shocking, I know, but proofreading was something that came naturally to me and I enjoyed it, so that's just what I pursued first. Other opportunities came later.

I eventually created Work-At-Home School to help people find their fit. There are even several courses in there that are designed to help you find your purpose and your passion. But—big but—it's easy to fool yourself into *feeling* like you're taking action, when really you're caught in the endless vortex of "research." If you refuse to get started on anything until you find the "perfect" thing you're passionate about, you're going to waste a *lot* of time—your most precious resource.

One Warning Before Moving Forward

Since time is your most precious resource, the last thing you want to do is waste it. The easiest way to waste time is to do nothing. Yet all kinds of perfectly capable people are too scared to even give anything a shot. They'd rather do nothing instead of face the uncertainty of something new. Before they even give themselves a chance, they give up on themselves. It's a choice, and they've already decided that it won't work... so what's the point in trying?

What these folks don't realize is that if they *do* nothing different in life, then they'll *get* nothing different in life. They live the same day every day—changing only the clothes on their backs. For these people, even the four-part test isn't enough. They first need to *think* differently. They need to level up their mindset.

It's sobering to realize the reason you haven't been living the life you deserve is because *you've* been holding *yourself* back. The biggest obstacle standing in your way might very well be *you*. If that's you, there's hope! This situation is not beyond repair. Our thoughts become our feelings, and from feelings stems *action*. Action is what gets you results. If you're not taking action, you can't expect results. If you fix your beliefs—what you think about yourself and your ability to make this work for you—your feelings will change, and so will your actions. And when your actions change... that's when the so-called "magic" happens: You get results!

That's why I spent so much time busting myths earlier in the book—so you could look those lies in the face, see them for what they are, and *stop believing them*. So you could take out the trash and replace it with truth. When you stop wasting brain energy on lies and looking for reasons you *can't* do something, you gain the brain space to believe the truth: You *can* do this.

It's all a choice, remember? You can *choose* to think differently. Is it easy? Far from it. Retraining your brain is hard, and it takes a lot of focus because our brains *fight* for sameness. It's human nature to resist change. That's why we feel so much fear crop up the moment we imagine doing something new—even if we know we'll become better in the process.

Too many intelligent people are too scared to invest even a *little* time and money into building a business. They all have *reasons.* Some of them have been burned by a scam or they've already shelled out a big chunk of change on education that didn't pan out. I've been there. That kind of experience can make anyone hesitate to take any risks. The $7,000 I spent to become a personal trainer is long gone, and it was *hard* for me to shift gears when I realized I didn't like it. *"I already spent all this money! It'd be a waste if I just gave up on it,"* I said. What I didn't realize is if I'd spent even one more day doing something I didn't like, *that'd be a waste, too.* A far worse one, at that!

Doing nothing often poses as "waiting for the right time" or "waiting until things settle down." And then there's the whole "waiting for the perfect opportunity" shenanigans. We delude ourselves into thinking "waiting" and even "researching" are productive activities. Waiting is a euphemism for doing nothing. Time passes, and you're not taking action.

In many cases, waiting is our way of passing the buck to someone or something else to change the situation so we feel comfortable enough to make a move. What's wrong with that, you ask? We give the responsibility of change to someone or something else. We remove ourselves from the equation. Thing is, you have no control over what someone else does; you only have control over what *you* do. If you sit and wait for all the ducks in your life to line up on their own before you go anywhere, you'll be waiting—*doing nothing*—for a long time. That's not what you want, is it? So the best solution is to effect your own change. Take action. Pick up one of those ducks and *run* with it. See what happens. More often than not, the rest of the ducks will follow!

Research is an even sneakier beast than waiting. Some research is good. Reading this book is considered research. Listening to the Work-At-Home Heroes podcast or reading posts in the Facebook group could also be considered research. It's necessary to explore options, but if you've been "researching" for many months or *years* and haven't taken any action, then something is wrong. You're *procrastinating*.

The most common cause for procrastination is simple fear. We do nothing so nothing bad will happen as a result. If we don't *do* anything, then there can't be any consequences... right?! Wrong. What we don't realize is that when nothing happens, *that* is what's bad—because what we *should* fear is getting to the end of our lives and realizing we let all that fear keep us from really living.

Taking action to improve your life is the most worthwhile investment you can make in yourself. Investing in yourself creates a ripple effect out into everyone whose lives you touch, whether that's your spouse and children, your parents, neighbors, or friends. The sooner you start investing in yourself, the better, even if you make mistakes along the way. We've already discussed the benefits of mistakes and failure—they're just a stepping stone on your journey; an opportunity to learn something new.

To be successful, you *must* take action with imperfect information. You can learn, adapt, and even completely change your path along the way. There's no perfect information and there's no perfect time. If you're waiting for perfect—or if you're waiting for comfort—you'll never do it. The perfect time is *now*. It's *always* now.

This will be true for the rest of your life. For example, it was scary when this book got picked up by an *actual* publisher. The fact that it would be in *actual* bookstores was scary. I couldn't help but think I wasn't ready. The book wasn't even done. I had four editors and twenty proofreaders read it, but I still wasn't happy with it. I still wasn't ready to publish it. It would have been much less scary to just share the book on my website and email list. Those people already know, like, and trust me. They'd be more inclined to like the book than people who don't know me yet. But I knew I'd never publish it if I waited to be ready because I'd never be "ready."

Everything I've ever done with my business I did before I felt "ready." The only real difference between the "me" I was and the "me" I am now is what's in my brain. It's my experience; it's my skills. I started something new—even though I thought I'd fail!—I made a bunch of mistakes, but I learned a ton and kept going even when I felt like giving up. Similarly, the only difference between the "you" you are now and the "you" you want to be is what's in *your* brain. Get curious about that. Get *excited* about that. How could your life improve if you learned something new and took action with that knowledge?

I still get nervous every time I start something new. Every single time. I think the same old self-doubting thoughts: Nobody's going to like this. Everyone will make fun of me. I'll make a fool out of myself. I'll screw something up and have to shut it down. It's always the same. Maybe you've felt that way before, too, and you might even feel that way now as you consider new possibilities for your life. I get it—because I've been there a lot. I'm probably there right now! Whatever you're scared of trying, I want to encourage you to do it anyway. Pick up that duck and run. Watch the other ducks follow!

It can be a struggle, of course. It's especially hard if you choose a path for the wrong reasons, get stuck in the "research" vortex, or try to wait until everything is "perfect" before you take the first step. But there's life beyond all that. It's scary; it's not always easy; but it's beautiful. Being able to look back on your journey a year from now with gratitude toward yourself for all the action you took despite your fear... that is priceless. That is growth. That is you writing your own income story. That is *living*.

The only cure for self-doubt is to take action. Move. *It's all a choice.* Choose something you're interested in. Choose something that seems to match your skills, interests, and desired lifestyle— knowing you can always choose something different later if you want to. Then, even if you don't feel ready, choose to *move*.

I like to use a simple analogy of buses and bus stops to illustrate how we can end the waiting game and become action takers. You can wait at the bus stop for years, but the "ready" bus will never come. It doesn't exist. So stop waiting for it. Just get on *any* bus that's moving, and go somewhere! (Take a duck with you; that'll be fun.) If you decide after a while that it's not a good fit, no biggie. Just get off that bus and choose another one. You'll always learn something from every ride, even if the ride is bumpy, makes you throw up, or doesn't pan out the way you thought it would.

You don't get traction without action. It's a law of physics. Waiting will do nothing. Waiting *is* doing nothing—and you're meant to do far more than nothing.

CHAPTER ELEVEN
Investing in Yourself and Your Future

Every business started with somebody investing time and/or money into it. Usually, it's both. For some people, that's bad news. If you're reading this right now and thinking you could be the exception; that you *could* make the money you want *without* investing anything or doing any work at all... you'll be sorely disappointed.

There's no such thing as a free lunch. The promise of getting something for nothing is what scammers peddle to lazy people. What did I promise you earlier in this book? I promised I'd never *sugarcoat* anything! Working at home is still work, but as I said: It's my favorite four-letter word.

Work can be fun, and using your brain to solve problems feels good. If we can disconnect "work" with the negative feelings we may have about it—either now or in the past—then the idea of *actually doing work* to make money isn't so scary or daunting anymore. Instead, we take responsibility and step into the power we have to design our lives the *exact* way we want. That's liberating, isn't it? Because you have the power of choice, *you're* in charge.

Lifelong learning and improvement of yourself is the wisest investment you can make. Lazy people are unhappy people. Stagnant, fixed-mindset folks who think nothing can ever change for them are unhappy, too. People who invest in improving themselves and the world by solving problems are happier, more fulfilled, and enjoy life *so much more* than those who spend their lives waiting and wishing.

You Are a Business

Before you can start making money at home like a boss, you first need to understand that you already *have* a business. You *are* a business right now. You own your brain and the knowledge and skills inside. That's all business is, after all: using skills to solve problems. It's transactional. You solve problems for someone and make money in exchange.

I know you might not *feel* like a business, but you are. Own it. See it from the perspective of the clients or customers you'd want to pay you for your services. What problems would they want you to solve? Why would they give you money for that? Clients want *value* from you. They want you to make their life better or easier in some way. They give you money for that value because they don't have the time or skills to do it themselves. Solving other people's problems = making money.

What if you're new? How can you possibly know what a client's problems are? This is a common hangup with newbies in the Work-At-Home Heroes community. They have an idea of the type of client they'd enjoy working with, but they don't know what services that client would need. Fortunately, this common problem has a very simple solution: *Ask* the client. Say, "Hey, what's the most annoying thing in your business that's keeping you from growing and/or making more money?" and just *see what they say.* Their answer will contain very specific clues to the skills you need to learn to be able to alleviate that annoyance—solve that *problem!*—in their business.

Let's take a look back at my proofreading business. My proofreading clients didn't want *clean words* from me, although that's what the work product was. Court reporters can make more money—in less time—by generating more transcripts and letting a proofreader clean them up. Proofreading takes a lot of time, and they don't make any money proofreading their own work. My clients' payments to me were investments in their business and income growth.

The same will be true for you. Your clients will give you money because they believe you're a good investment for them in some way. But if you don't invest in yourself, it'll be awfully hard to find clients willing to invest in you. Other people who do invest in themselves will outshine you because they'll surpass your skill level and offer more than you can. Similarly, if you don't invest in efficient software and tools to perform your work, clients may get frustrated with you and move on.

Finally, the online universe is expanding faster than the actual universe. If you don't invest in ongoing education—courses, coaching, and networking with peers—you'll be left behind. That's how fast the internet moves. Ask anyone who got a computer science degree in the nineties who thought their bachelor's degree alone would carry them through to retirement.

Don't Be a Know-It-All

You don't know everything already. Don't make the mistake of thinking you do. The best business track for you is something where you can use skills you have—but something you are willing to grow and develop.

In no industry is the know-it-all mindset more prevalent than proofreading. A solid 85% of students who begin my proofreading courses believe they already know how to proofread. *"All I need to know is how to market myself and find clients!"* they tell me, naïvely. It's not their fault; I felt that way too when I started my blog! It wasn't until I got into the thick of teaching proofreading did I realize what I *didn't* know. It was a wakeup call for sure, and that's eventually what the former know-it-alls tell me: *"I didn't know what I didn't know!"*

They had blind spots. We all do. The best of us—the most successful of us—recognize those blind spots. We *know* we don't already know everything. We adopt a mindset that we'll never be done learning. Not only is this the recipe for continued personal growth, it's also good for business. When clients see you investing in yourself; when they see you hungry for more and soaking up new skills like a sponge, they gain confidence in you, too.

I'm not just shooting the breeze here; I'm speaking from firsthand experience. Nearly my entire virtual team is made up of students who've completed at least one of my online courses. I hand-selected them based on their performance *and* their attitude. Whenever I post job openings, I'm very clear on what skills I need for the problems I have. The people who respond and tell me what part of the job description they *won't, don't,* or *can't* do… I delete their emails immediately.

Never, ever email a potential client/employer in response to a job post to tell them what you *won't, don't,* or *can't* do. Don't respond at all if you don't fit the description and aren't willing to learn. Attitude can sometimes fill in gaps in your current skill set. Some of my best hires have been people who were honest about what skills they didn't yet have, but their willingness to learn and positive attitude made me hire them anyway.

Clients Can Sense Your Attitude

If you have a chip on your shoulder, believe you already know everything, or try to cut corners, clients can sense it. I can sense it from a mile away if someone has no idea what they're doing and is just trying to make a quick buck. Unfortunately I had to learn that skill through experience. If you're worried about clients passing on you for someone else, you can alleviate that worry by committing to excellence. Commit to investing in yourself, lifelong learning, and keeping up with the shifting tides of technology. Commitment is a choice. *It's all a choice.*

Investing in your own success takes time and work, and that's not something everyone is willing to do. That's why I'm never worried about the availability of work for freelancers. In our modern world, laziness and the entitlement mentality have taken over. A large majority of people —especially in the West—don't believe they should have to learn or do *anything* differently in order to have a better life. Instead, they believe it's the government's responsibility to take care of them and improve their quality of life.

Investing time and money is also too "risky" for many people— mostly because they feel overwhelmed and believe they have to do it all overnight. A train doesn't leave the station at full speed. Momentum requires movement, but it doesn't have to be *fast* movement. Attempting to do it all at once at lightning speed is the fastest way to a flat tire on the road to success. *Move slowly.*

Start with what you have and allow your brain to adjust, then slowly add more. When you're baking a cake, what happens when you quickly dump all the dry ingredients into the wet ingredients? Flour gets everywhere. It's frustrating, isn't it? *Move slowly.* The cake will turn out better.

Finally, learn to be okay with never being "done." It'd be awfully boring to be "done." Sure; endless self-improvement and problem solving can get tiring, but that's why you take a break or a vacation. If you start this journey thinking there'll eventually come a time where you can just kick up your feet and let the money roll in, you're setting yourself up for failure. If you try to find the cheapest solutions to things instead of the *best* ones to get your clients the *best* results, the same will happen.

If you stop investing in yourself, you'll hit a skill ceiling. You'll hit a productivity ceiling. Limiting your skills and productivity means you'll *definitely* hit an income ceiling. Let me remind you that there is no *real* limit to skills, productivity, or income other than the ones we place on ourselves. The most effective way to avoid creating those ceilings in your life is to wisely invest time and/or money in three key areas.

I'll hammer out the details on each of those areas now...

Invest in Skill Development

Simply put, if your skills are mediocre, your income will be mediocre. Improving your skills is an investment in Future You. It allows you to offer more services, charge more money, and work more efficiently. These help you serve more customers. The most successful freelancers constantly improve their skills.

You can develop skills by investing time or money in courses, books, or even local workshops. There are countless places to find online or offline courses. Look for free YouTube tutorials. Take courses like the ones I offer through Proofread Anywhere or Work-At-Home School. If you have trouble finding courses, check out the Resources page for this book. I've included a bunch of places to find online courses for almost *any* skill.

RESOURCE PAGE

WorkAtHomeSchool.com/BookResources

Just keep in mind that it's not the course, book, or resource itself that's valuable—it's what you *do* with it. Information is useless without implementation, so simply enrolling in some training will get you nowhere.

Invest in Community

Even if you invest oodles of time and money into developing your skills and become a business superstar, the road can be rough if you're alone all the time! Loneliness is a real struggle for many work-at-home heroes. Community is the remedy against it.

Community doesn't have to happen in "real life" all the time either. Of course, if you can get plugged into a live community of like-minded people in your hometown, that'll give you a dimension of human connection you can't duplicate online. That said, online communities are also excellent places to forge friendships and to network with your peers.

Community provides the business-building blocks of support, accountability, and direction we all need to build sustainable income from home. The Work-At-Home Heroes group on Facebook is an excellent example of a supportive community of people with the common goal of writing their own income stories by using skills to solve problems. If you're feeling downtrodden or burnt out, a few minutes spent in there has the same potency as a nice, cold glass of water on a hot summer day. See for yourself!

Invest in the Right Tools to Set Up and Operate Your Business

Once you've got the skills development down—and you've got trustworthy people in your corner to support you—the third major area you'll need to invest in is *tools*. I'm talking about things like a website, bookkeeping software (Excel spreadsheets are a no-no!), and up-to-date, functioning equipment to perform your services.

It's tempting to go cheap when you're starting out—for example, you may be tempted to go with a free website that has a yourname.subdomain.com URL. Don't do this! Go to the website building tutorial on the book resource page (WorkAtHomeSchool.

com/BookResources) and use that to set up a *real* website without spending a lot of money.

Although I didn't go with a free website, one big mistake I made when just starting out was refusing to pay for a premium theme for my WordPress website. I used a free theme instead, which gave my website a tacky, unprofessional feel. Because I had a fixed mindset and was sure my new venture would fail, I was incredibly hesitant to invest money into my new business. It was like pulling teeth to get me to invest any money into building a better website, but once I did, I saw an almost *immediate* increase in my income.

Earlier in this chapter, I said that clients can sense it when you cut corners. Marketing a business with a free website is a dead giveaway that you're too cheap to invest $30 a year for basic website hosting—it begs the question: What else are you too cheap to invest in? A reliable internet connection? Backup for important files? There's no arguing that a real website emanates a much more "legit" vibe than a free one.

You might be reading this and thinking, *"Hey, Caitlin; I get it. You've got to spen— er, invest money to make money. But what if I don't have any money to invest?"* If that's you, don't despair. There are other options! I know dozens of people who exchange services with other budding freelancers. If you're great at writing, find a web designer who needs to build their portfolio and offer to write content for a few of his or her clients' websites in exchange for their help building a great-looking website for you. Teamwork makes the dream work!

Declutter your attic, garage, and hall closet and look for items you can sell online. You might be surprised what you've got lying around that could be worth $10, $20, or even hundreds of dollars. It all adds up.

One warning, though. A lot of people use "investing in tools" as an excuse to buy toys or random stuff they don't *need* to set up or operate their business. A brand-new desk. New paint in their office. A sparkly pink laptop case. I've seen people spend *months* "getting ready" to start their business. They think they need to have the perfect office environment before they can make money. Newsflash… remember my no-A/C apartment in Chile? I made tens of thousands of dollars working from a *futon* in that place. (Don't ask me why I didn't choose a different Airbnb; my husband is still mad at me about that…) All you need for a basic business to function is a working computer and a reliable internet connection.

The tendency many newbies have to spend lots of time and money on unnecessary stuff is quite similar to the endless vortex of "research" you read about earlier. It's procrastination, and it stems from simple fear. You subconsciously spend time and money on that unnecessary stuff to postpone what you fear: failure. Once everything is *perfect*—and there's absolutely no chance you can fail—*then* you'll start. The longer it takes to make things perfect, the longer you can postpone failure. This can go on forever, just like the endless vortex of research. So forget about all the perfection and the unnecessary frills.

No frills… just skills. But don't even *think* about using that corny mantra to justify a lame yourname.subdomain.com website! A real website is not an option; it's a necessity—*if* you want to be legit.

On the topic of websites, I've got a riveting tale of a recent personal struggle in that domain (pun intended)…

Why I Spent $2,500 on a Domain Name

In July 2017, the idea for Work-At-Home School was swimming around in my brain, and I needed to secure a domain so it could live someplace official online. Obviously, WorkAtHomeSchool.com was perfect, but someone already owned it... and wanted *$2,500* for it. Ouch.

Up to that point, the most I'd ever spent on a domain name was $15, tops. I've always been pretty frugal with my spending. Let's just say if we're ever at Nordstrom together and we get separated, you'll find me in the clearance section! So I was chewing my nails over whether I should buy something "second best" for $15... or buy *exactly* what I wanted for $2,500.

On one hand, I thought, I could do a lot for my business with an extra $2,485 in my pocket. On the other, for $2,500 I could buy—nay; *invest in*—the perfect domain name for Work-At-Home School. It was perfect, after all!

I felt so torn that I posted about it on Facebook and got loads of wise advice from a lot of people I trusted:

Stephanie said, "Get the thing that works best the first time around."

Brooke said, "Get what you want. The cheaper one will likely end up costing you in the long run."

Bev said, "Do it right the first time, and you'll have no regrets."

I had lived a lot of my life with a clearance-rack mindset. My friends helped me realize I was not *spending* money on this domain. I was *investing* money in my project. The investor mindset is tough sometimes. Even *I* struggled with it with WorkAtHomeSchool.com and needed my community to help me snap out of it!

It's shocking how many people—without even a second thought—will take out $100,000 *or more* in loans for a degree that'll cap their income potential and tie them to a desk for decades. Many of those same folks will then put up a ton of resistance toward investing in skills courses they could use to *uncap* their income. They can't justify parting with even a few hundred dollars for a course—even if that investment would allow them to earn far more than that for the rest of their lives.

Don't let that be you. Skills—and the knowledge and ability to monetize them—are the *real* job security. At this point in the book, you *know* this. You know you can lose your job and income at a moment's notice, but barring any catastrophic brain injury, you cannot lose the skills you've mastered.

You can always learn more skills to earn more money, and there is no better time than now to do it. Life isn't a dress rehearsal, y'know? This is *it*. This is your life, and you're worth the investment.

CHAPTER TWELVE
Real Wealth (and the Scarcest Resource on Earth)

G rowing up, I always thought if I ever became a millionaire, I'd do what "rich" people did. In my mind, that meant spending tons of money on a fancy house, clothes, a car (or six), and throwing lavish parties. While I did splurge on a beautiful house and my dream car, the truth is that most new people I meet—and the ones I run into in my travels—probably think I'm a broke drifter. I do *not* look the part of a millionaire.

Most millionaires *don't* spend money on luxury vacations, clothing, houses, and cars. As I grew my own net worth and got to know other millionaires, I learned money only matters to a certain point. After that point, your focus shifts away from money... and moves toward *meaning*. You start thinking more about managing your *time* well. How you invest your time will have a greater impact on the quality of your life than any amount of money. A meaningful, healthy life is *real* wealth.

A lot of people who *look* wealthy aren't wealthy at all. Have you ever wondered how a neighbor or coworker can afford the car they drive? You might have thought they inherited money or have a spouse who makes good money, and that's possible, I guess—but it's more likely they *can't* afford the car. It's far easier to look rich than it is to become rich. People who appear wealthy often live paycheck to paycheck and have a *negative* net worth. They're drowning in debt!

Most people with a net worth of more than a million dollars actually live well *below* their means. That's often how they accumulated their wealth in the first place. They still clip coupons, buy stuff off craigslist, shop the clearance rack, and go to matinees. I do all of these things! My philosophy is that there's never a good reason to spend unwisely—and some coupons are as good as free money!

When it comes to spending and saving, the sweet spot is in the middle. Live a relatively simple life so you can build wealth. Buy your dream house and car only when you can comfortably afford it. You don't want to be "house poor," but don't deprive yourself unnecessarily either. A quality environment can boost your mood and productivity, so think twice before settling for the cheap 400-square-foot apartment with no air conditioning if you can easily afford better! Similarly, if you're holding on to that 2001 Honda that breaks down every week, that's costing you time—the scarcest, most valuable resource on Earth.

Even though I'm financially independent now, for the longest time I saw *money* as a scarce resource. I went through life thinking there was only so much money to go around. Some people had it; others didn't. I was just one of the ones in the "didn't" category. That mindset helped me save a lot of money but also wasted a lot of precious time. I was afraid to hire help when I needed it because "why pay someone when I can do it myself for free?" Thing is, it's *not* free if doing it myself costs me *time*.

"Free" is all about perspective. Why spend three hours a week cleaning up my yard just to save $100, when I *could* spend that same three hours creating a new video workshop that could generate many thousands of dollars? I'd rather give $100 to someone who makes their living helping people clean up their yards! I call that investing in the local economy.

The most valuable lesson I've learned in the last decade is how valuable time is. As a result, I now trade money for more time any chance I get. I invested thousands of dollars in full-body laser hair removal so I didn't have to spend so much time shaving anymore. I've had my eyebrows tattooed so I don't have to groom them nearly as often. I started getting eyelash extensions put on once a month because I used to spend *hours* every week applying and removing mascara. Perhaps those things sound a little vain, but I estimate that I've added *at least* 10 hours of time to my life every month because of those investments. That's 120 hours a year! #goodatmath

Think about it for a moment. How many times have *you* wished you had an extra hour in your day? Forget about personal grooming time; what if you could take back even a few hours of your time every weekday by cutting out commuting, pointless meetings, and time spent "looking busy" just so you can clock 40 hours? Over 10 years, that would be like getting back more than 200 days of your life. Over a 35-year career, it would be like adding *two extra years* to your life.

What would you do with all that extra time?

Final Words on Investing in Yourself

My entire world changed when I started investing in building my skills and buying more time. I built a multimillion-dollar business from scratch. Now I realize the *only* thing that stood between me and massive income was my skills, and I hope by now you're starting to see that the same is true for you! By now you know I'm not special, and I didn't just "get lucky." I didn't start running some scam. There's nothing scammy about skills. I learned how to do more stuff to help more people, and as a result I made more money.

The *only* thing standing between *you* and more income is *your* skills—and how *you* develop and market them. Most of the skills you need aren't hard to learn. At first, learning skills can seem intimidating because you haven't mastered them yet. You can't expect yourself to feel confident in something you haven't mastered. In the same way you won't get traction without action, you won't get confidence without mastery.

That first client might only pay you a few hundred dollars, but that's all you need for that precious momentum. All it takes to start a fire is a single spark. Stay consistent and allow the momentum to build and before you know it, you could very well be earning more money than you ever thought possible—right from your couch.

Solve other people's problems, and you'll earn money. Make solving other people's problems your focus, and your own problems naturally disappear. The late Zig Ziglar used to say something that illustrates this concept well. "You can have everything in life you want, if you will just help enough other people get what they want." That's all there is to it, and the opportunities are limitless—

especially with the powerful tool we call the internet. As long as there are people in the world with problems to solve, there will *always* be opportunities to earn money!

Some people reject this mindset. Instead of putting other people's problems first, they put themselves first—and prey on unsuspecting individuals any way they can just to increase their bottom line. They solve *zero* problems and instead create problems; even financial ruin in the worst cases. Who are they? These people are *scammers*, and in the next chapter you'll learn how to sniff 'em out—and shut 'em down.

The Scams and You

CHAPTER THIRTEEN
Getting Real about Scams

"*Everything's a scam!*" I hear or read this statement from someone at least once a day. I also hear the myth perpetuated that in order to make money at home, your only option is to buy into some kind of "business in a box" and push products on your friends and family. None of that is true. In fact, these rumors probably got started by a handful of disgruntled someones who bought into a slick sales pitch one night in someone's living room—or they got sucked into a sleazy ad that promised they could "make money fast."

I remember the first time I got scammed. I was nine years old, and on the last day of fourth grade I gave this girl named Amanda a dollar for "flower perfume." I don't recall smelling or even seeing a sample of said flower perfume, but somehow I wanted it bad enough that I coughed up a paper George Washington for it. Guess what happened? I never saw Amanda again. Nine-year-old me got scammed out of my hard-earned weed-pulling money!

Beyond the mysterious flower perfume, there are *many* scams that prey on people's naïveté, and I hate it because it gives the legitimate stuff a limp from the start. The scams shouldn't deter you from trying; you've just got to get smart and know what's legit and what's not. Working for a company isn't necessary, either—that's just one of *thousands* of legitimate ways to make it happen.

Many people create their own work-at-home careers. They use a skill they're good at to sell a product or service with predictable profits. Paving your *own* way is my personal favorite pathway to work-at-home success.

The key to creating your own work-at-home job *isn't* to cram yourself into the mold of what someone else is doing or to become a Jack/Jill of all trades. The key is to start with *one* skill and build from there. *Slowly.* You do no favors for anyone by rushing or doing haphazard work because you think it'll earn you money faster. For me, my one skill was proofreading. For you, it could be writing or helping a blogger answer emails from readers. *One* skill.

You don't have to peddle products you don't care about, either. Again, this *can be* true, but it doesn't have to be. You could certainly sell products from home—especially if you really like them! You can even create your *own* products and sell them on your *own* online store. Is this more labor intensive than selling someone else's products? Sure. But the profit margins are much higher, and you have much more control over how you market and sell your products.

Whatever you choose, know that *you're not stuck with it forever* if you end up not liking it. It's a skill, not a life sentence or worse, a death sentence—learning skills won't kill you! Instead of making "perfect" your goal, look for something that's good enough to start.

The Elephant in the Room

Before we move on into a deeper discussion of scams, let's address the, erm... *elephant* in the room. I alluded to it in the first section of this chapter when I mentioned pushing products on your friends and family. These are sometimes called network marketing or multilevel marketing companies. I'll refer to them as MLMs for short.

I want to make it clear that I rarely, if ever, recommend getting involved in MLMs. It's not that I think they're scams, although some of them are. The people who make the most money with MLMs are the ones who treat it like a recruiting company. They get their friends, family, and strangers to sign up as salespeople. The ones who simply sell the MLMs' products are *rarely* the ones making big money.

Many people choose MLM opportunities because *they seem easy*. Just sell this high-quality product to your friends and family and get a couple of 'em to sign up and sell too! It's *easy*, they say! Based on what I know about marketing (which is a *lot* and that's largely the reason my students are so successful), a big part of the reason people new to MLM don't succeed is that they focus too much on the product instead of the problem it solves. Nobody cares about the bells and whistles of X, Y, or Z product; they care about how that product will improve their life. The bigger problem a product solves, the easier it will be to sell (to the right people, that is).

They also don't understand how to network online *beyond* their immediate sphere of influence, and that's why many of the MLMers you see in your Facebook feed are so annoying. One day you see great photos of kids, vacations, and funny cat videos and the next day? *"Hey, I just started a new business selling this awesome widget!"* The next thing you know, you're in a Facebook group about sexy lips and getting invited to online trunk shows.

It's such a turn-off to be constantly marketed to by friends and family, isn't it? So don't do it to your peeps. There is a better way to sell products—and that's by using the internet to expand your network via paid or organic marketing. You can find people far more likely to buy from you than your grandmother. You do not *have* to ask your Uncle Ned if he's interested in buying a body wrap. If you do get involved in an MLM, promise me you'll make sure to learn marketing skills like copywriting, audience targeting, advertising, and network *outside* of your personal Facebook profile.

Nothing about working from home has to be shady. Copywriter Melody DiCroce once thought working from home meant jobs from "the backs of magazines or on craigslist." She even "tried one or two of these types of jobs early on and never made any money." Thanks to the internet, Melody found reputable people teaching how to work from home. She learned she didn't have to sell her soul to work from home. That was "completely life-changing" for her. She worked hard and grew her copywriting side hustle. She then left her day job to freelance while sailing the Western Caribbean on her sailboat.

Again, nothing against MLMs in general. They're just not a great fit for most people, and, yes, some are complete scams. If you find one that really piques your interest, take a closer look. Is it something in which you're dying to get involved? If not, you probably have better options. Do you need to fill your garage with products before you can start making money? If so, I'd run away fast. If you decide to go for it, keep your guard up and know that it's not a life sentence if you don't like it—it's okay to get off the bus and change directions.

CHAPTER FOURTEEN
Spotting and Avoiding Scams

The internet is rife with scammers preying on people. My team and I have heard a lot of stories from students who've been burned by scams. That's why this chapter breaks down scams in detail—because if you don't see them coming, the scams could burn *you!*

With so many scammers, it can be downright hard to spot the legit stuff. A few scams have been around a long time. These in particular *really* get under my skin:

- Envelope stuffing

- Email processing

- Home typing

- Pretty much anything that markets using a 900 call-in number. Stay away if you see, "Just call this 1-900 number for more information."

The way envelope stuffing usually works is pretty simple. People see an ad about making money stuffing envelopes from home.

They envision working while their baby sleeps or while watching TV. When they call to ask about the opportunity, the person on the other line says it's easy to get started; all they need to do is buy a "starter kit" that contains detailed instructions. They pay and receive the kit… which instructs them to stuff envelopes advertising envelope-stuffing jobs. If that sounds scammy, it's because it *is* scammy. They stuff envelopes full of information on how to make money stuffing envelopes. The idea is to dupe more people into buying a "starter kit" to continue the cycle. A pointless scam.

"Email processing" is nothing but a new spin on envelope stuffing. Although it might sound legit to "just process email" all day, it's not. You pay $25 to learn how to post the same ad you responded to and get other people to pay you $25. It's ridiculous. When I see this posted by someone I know, I immediately jump to the comments to let them know what a crock it is. Call me crazy, but I'm just being a good friend.

Home typing is another sell-nothing scam. You pay money to receive a disk. On the disk is a set of instructions telling you to create ads about home typing. The idea is to get people to pay *you* for the same instructions. Scam.

"Simply Call This 1-900 Number for More Information" ads are the worst! With many of these, there's no real opportunity. You don't even get the chance to resell the "opportunity" like the other scams. The 1-900 numbers make their money just by getting you—and keeping you—on the phone!

I've gotten hundreds of emails from people who got burned. Some share detailed accounts of getting scammed by "email processing" and "recruitment" schemes. It's always the same story.

They pay $25 to learn how to get $25 from people by teaching them how to get $25 from people. They sell nothing. They buy and sell lame scripts and "techniques" to con people into sending $25 for the same lame scripts. These ads get people because they make it super simple to call or email them and sell you on something for $25 or so. It's a low enough amount that people send it thinking they have little to lose.

Scammers care only about solving their own problem and increasing their bottom line. They prey on people looking for an easy way to earn money from home. None of them sell anything. None add value to anyone. These scams are *nothing* but ways to get money from you.

Other than the obviousness of the above known work-from-home scams, how can you know something's a scam? How can you separate the facts from the crap? Here are my top tips to help you.

Tip No. 1: Make sure there are no overly lofty promises that you'll earn money with little to no work.

Be very wary if someone *guarantees* you'll make money simply by buying into the program. Truckloads of MLMs are notorious for these promises. "All you have to do is sell these products and sign other people up underneath you. Then just watch the cash flow in!" Heh. If only it were *that* easy!

Legitimate people will let you know what to expect and make their promises clear. My proofreading courses guarantee that you'll have everything you need to *work* as a proofreader: the right tools, resources, practice, and support. I will never, *ever* put a blanket guarantee you'll *earn money* simply by paying for or even completing the course. In fact, I guarantee you'll earn *nothing* if all you do is take the course.

That's the key difference. Taking a course or buying a program will never be enough by itself. The internet is cool, but it's not magical. You'll never "automagically" become a money-making success by *taking* a course or program. You make money by *implementing* on what you learn. Information is useless without implementation. #brokenrecord

The same is true with this book or Work-At-Home School. I can teach you *everything* I know, but you'll make zero dollars and zero cents unless *you* put in the work. I'm not a wizard! What can I say? I'm a Hogwarts reject.

Building a career working from home is bona fide hard work. Anyone promising you the opposite of that is probably trying to *just get* your money, not *help you make* money.

Bottom line is if it sounds too good to be true, it probably is. Stay away.

Tip No. 2: Contact the person behind the snazzy website and stalk them online.

If you're considering a program or opportunity of any sort, make sure you get to know the person behind the product. This holds whether it's an eBook, a course, or even some kind of franchise.

Before purchasing anything education-related online, always send an email or make a call (if possible) to the person in charge. I actually ask people to reply back to me in each lesson of my free mini course at Proofread Anywhere. Lots of folks are absolutely *floored* by this but to me, it's part of the job—my favorite part, actually! I know how annoying it is when I try to reach out to someone (or a company) online and can't get to them, so I go out of my way to be *approachable* and *available*. My door is always open.

Anyone trying to sell you something as pivotal as an online course *should* be available to help. If not them, then a trusted member of their team (because we have to sleep sometimes!). It should be easy to get in touch with them or a trusted person on their team. If it's hard or impossible to find a contact form, that's not a good sign. If you email several times with no response, that's also not a good sign.

Stalk the instructor on social media, too. Look them up on Facebook. Find them on LinkedIn. Google the heck out of them. Is the general consensus about them positive or negative? What kinds of content are they posting? What kind of person are they? What are people saying about them? Are the majority of their students happy? What are the complainers saying? Are they saying, "I worked my tail off for a year and didn't make any progress"? Or are they saying, "This is too much work and I didn't get rich overnight"? Are they featured in the media for their work? Can you find any interviews of them?

If your research doesn't bring up a positive result—or it brings up no result at all—there's a good chance you can find something better elsewhere. There's also a chance what they're pitching isn't legitimate or the instructor's a poser. I know; I know; we're going back to middle school for a moment, but there are a lot of posers out there! "Posers" on the internet take someone else's "good idea" and try to market it as their own. There are also many cookie-cutter "coaching coaches" out there. Be on the lookout for these people. These people teach others how to become *coaches who coach coaches to coach coaches*. Coach them on what? Coaching coaches. I know! It's dumb.

Before you spend a penny to learn how to build a business, google the instructor's name with the word "scam" after it, and take a look at the first 1-3 pages of results. Read the reviews—the good and the bad—and make your decision based on what you see. (Go ahead; google "Caitlin Pyle scam." I know you want to!)

Be sure to *read* the reviews, too. Don't just look at star ratings. A bad review might be what's not legitimate—not the product itself. The majority of my 1-star reviews come from people who have never taken one of my courses. I've gotten bad reviews from people who are mad that I don't give away my courses for free. I've gotten bad reviews from people who don't like my ads on Facebook. I've gotten bad reviews from people who said I send too many emails or—get this!—found a typo in an email and used that as a reason not to enroll. They leave a review not based on a course, but based on *me* not meeting their expectation of perfection. Nobody's perfect—not even proofreaders.

Don't let a snazzy website fool you. Make sure you get in touch with and research the person behind the website, including me! I've made it easy for you to check me out. I put all my info on the Resources page. You'll find all my websites, social profiles, and contact information there, and of course… you can google me!

Tip No. 3: Read the warnings and disclaimers—and there should be honest warnings and disclaimers.

Working at home isn't for everyone. It's hard work. If a site advertises their offer as a ticket to freedom *without* having to do any work, get off that site fast! Remember what you learned about scammers earlier in this chapter. They prey on people by painting their product as an *easy* way out. They want you to think they have a magic pill.

Look for sites that are up front about what they offer. It shouldn't have very much fine print—especially as it pertains to the details of the offer. If it's a course, can you download a syllabus that breaks down what each unit and module include? On the sales page where you can read all the details on the offer, is there a list of who is *not* a good fit for it—or just gobs of sparkly words designed to pull you in? You actually want to see some clear language targeting people who are not a good fit. This is called "disqualifying" language. Disqualifiers keep low-quality people who are looking for the mythical cure-all *out* of a program or community.

Let me give you an example of some disqualifying language straight from the enrollment page for my general proofreading online course:

> **❝** Enrolling in a course doesn't entitle you to success. This isn't a get-rich-quick course. Proofreading isn't a world where you go through a course and then have

clients waiting for you at the end. It takes time and a lot of hard work to build a business. It's rewarding, for sure—but if you're not up for it, just don't enroll. I mean it—if you're just looking for something to rush through and then refuse to put in the effort to build a quality reputation in the proofreading world, turn around now! This course isn't for you.

See what I mean? Even on a sales page—which *is* designed to sell—there should always be honest language like this.

The Bottom Line on Spotting Scams

Legitimate opportunities don't make lofty promises and make it clear that you'll actually have to *work* to succeed. You should be able to *easily* get in touch with the owner of the company or a member of his/her team to get answers to your questions. Lastly, the sales page shouldn't be littered with the colorful stuff designed to dazzle and pull in anyone and everyone—it should also include disqualifying language, warnings, and clear disclaimers to weed out people who aren't a good fit. If you check an opportunity against the tips in this section, you can safely proceed. Proceed with caution, but proceed.

Now that you know the clear differences between scams and legit opportunities, you're far less likely to waste precious time and money by falling prey to a scammer. Let that empower you to go forth on this journey with more confidence in yourself to choose wisely. In this case, knowledge truly is power!

CHAPTER FIFTEEN
How *You* Can Avoid Becoming a Scam

We busted the scammers, but did you know that you could inadvertently *become* a scam yourself?

Too many people start with big dreams, thinking they'll become millionaires in no time. There's nothing wrong with being optimistic, but you're *not* going to become a millionaire in a week. You're not going to become a millionaire in a month. In fact, the vast majority of people won't even become millionaires in a decade.

There are many reasons for that, but the bottom line is to become wealthy, you need to help a lot of people. Notice I didn't say you need to *sell to* a lot of people. You'll need to *help* them. If you keep your focus on solving other people's problems—instead of merely making money—your money problems will solve themselves. Nobody will give you business or money unless you help them first.

People reach out to me with questions about my proofreading courses all the time. Most of the time, these people ask me to train them and are willing to invest in my courses. But sometimes…

sometimes the emails are *full* of typos and entitlement mentality. It's clear these folks are *not* a good fit. They ask things like "When will you be sending me work?" or "When do I get paid if I sign up for this?"

When—or if—I reply to these emails, I say something like this: "We don't give people money or give people jobs. We teach people how to generate income *for themselves* by learning and implementing skills. They become self-sufficient and able to earn income for a lifetime. We'd have to charge a lot more if we did all the work for you." Their responses to my frankness are usually something to the effect of "I ain't payin' to get no job," or "Education should be free." Here's my personal favorite: "I knew it was too good to be true. Scam."

These people just want money. They expect *me* to *give* them free money, free training, or introductions to clients. And when I say no, they call *me* a scam... which makes no sense.

Having that kind of entitlement mentality, however, is exactly how *any* of us can become a scam if we're not careful. In many cases, we've *learned* to have this mindset in very legitimate circumstances, like school, sports teams—perhaps even our own families taught us that our own well-being is the *government's* responsibility instead of our own.

I've had the entitlement mentality! Remember how I told you I believed that because I went to college that I was entitled to a well-paying job? That's what was hammered into my brain all through school as I was growing up: Go to college, and you'll get a great job. That happened to many of us, and it's not getting better for younger generations. Everybody wins these days. Trophies for *everyone!*

So how can you avoid being a scam? Two ways. First, rid yourself of every last bit of the entitlement mentality. Be willing to work your way up from the bottom. Invest in building relationships and solving problems instead of making money your top priority. Do good work, serve your clients well, and you'll earn their trust—and referrals.

Second, have realistic expectations. Don't quit your job today and expect to be able to replace your income within a week. You're human, and learning new skills will take time. Accept that and enjoy the process. Especially if the fear of failure has you in its snare, starting small is very safe. You can build your income on the side and quit your day job once you have enough side income to work with.

That's how to avoid becoming a scammer. It's all in your mindset. What's your priority? Is it solving problems for other people… or making money for yourself? I know at this point in the book, you already know the answer! Even if you think it'll help you meet your goals faster, cutting corners or taking shortcuts can come back to bite you.

Summing It Up

Be wary of lofty promises to get rich quick or make money without any work. A legitimate opportunity should put *you* first. Course instructors—or whoever is advertising an offer—should be easy to contact. Honesty and disqualifying language should be present on their sales pages to help them filter out people who aren't a good fit for their offer.

To avoid becoming a scam yourself, steer clear of the entitlement mentality. Have realistic expectations for your progress. Take your time, and when it comes to your work, always put other people first.

Cutting corners is for suckers, and that's not you, Boo.

Identifying Your Best Options

CHAPTER SIXTEEN
The Fastest Way to Start

Some people need a little cash infusion to get started. I get it. Money might be tight. Bills don't stop coming just because you want 'em to, either. Understand that it's totally acceptable—and common!—to need to make a little money first before investing in courses, training, or equipment. If that's you, lean in. Other people want to test out the freelancing world to see if they like it. Dip a toe in, so to speak. If *that's* you, pull up a chair.

Here's a little secret. If you're willing to step out of your comfort zone, anyone reading this can start making money relatively quickly—possibly even before the end of the book! In fact, there's a foolproof way to make money fast that hardly anyone teaches. Want to know it? Market a skill you *already* have to people you *already* know. *GASP!*

Crazy, right?! That's it? Yep, that's it. The simplest, quickest way to make extra money—*without* investing money or time into training—is to market a skill you already have to people you already know.

To be clear, I *don't* mean you should plaster spammy ads all over everyone's timeline or blast them with incessant private messages. The technique I'll share in just a moment is much more subtle than that. It's designed to put out some "feelers" *without* annoying your social network.

"But I don't have any skills, Caitlin! It's hopeless for me." Nope. We all have skills. Most of us don't even recognize skills for what they are because they come so naturally to us. Sometimes in-demand skills masquerade as everyday tasks. You already have marketable skills even if you don't think you do. The trick is finding those skills and then deciding which one to pursue. Here's how to do that.

How to Find Your Marketable Skills

Simply put, an in-demand, marketable skill is anything you can do to make people's lives easier. That can be either virtually or in person. It doesn't have to be anything complicated. You don't have to cure cancer or invent a new theory or product. What are some ways you help people save time or money? *Those* are things people pay for every day. Those are things *I* pay for every day!

Almost anyone can run errands, do laundry, organize or clean people's homes or offices. Almost anyone can scan or file paperwork, cook food, pet sit, or walk dogs, too. These are skills I—and many other business owners—personally pay thousands of dollars per month for. Why? Because if I spent all my time doing those tasks just because I *can* do them, then I'd have far less time and energy to be there for my tribe and my team. Outsourcing tasks someone else can easily do expands my ability to do more for them—and for myself, too.

As simple as these things sound, I assure you there's *solid* demand for them. I pay a young woman $2,700 per month to help me full-time with errands, laundry, housekeeping, grocery shopping, cooking, pet care, organizing... you name it; she does it—without complaint! She will even find problems to solve for me that I didn't even know existed. For example, instead of keeping my spices randomly stored in all-different-sized containers, she suggested organizing them alphabetically and investing in spice jars with labels to make each spice easier to find. I gave her a big thumbs up on the project and loved the result!

You might be thinking there's *no way* you'd do any of those tasks for someone else. If that's you, and you want to make extra money and start building work-at-home income, then I'm going to ask you one question: *How bad do you want it?* Because here's the thing. Tons of people *want* to make extra money, but far fewer are willing to *work* for it. Similarly, lots of people *want* to lose weight or improve their relationship with their spouse, but far fewer are willing to *do* anything to get that result. They think it should be easy. They'd rather sit there for *hours* scrolling through get-rich-quick schemes, reading about crash diets, and sifting through articles looking for "tricks" to a better relationship. What a waste of time!

It all goes back to mindset. There's a rampant misunderstanding of what it takes to make money. The average Joe *doesn't connect the dots* between solving problems and earning income. That's why that theme recurs so often throughout this book. You *must* compute and accept this concept to be successful. Money doesn't grow on trees, and you won't make more of it just by wishing, hoping, or wanting to. If you're in a situation where you need to make money now before you can invest in building more profitable skills, then the worst thing you can do to remedy that situation is to be *picky* about what you're willing to do to make that happen.

It can be tempting to turn your nose up at opportunities that seem to be at the bottom of the totem pole. Answering customer service calls or emails may not be your dream job, but it *can* be a stepping stone toward your dream—if you are humble enough to take that step. Even taking a step onto an ugly stepping stone is far better than not taking a step at all. A step is a step, and every step is an opportunity to learn something new. The job you may feel is "beneath" you can actually elevate you. So what if it only pays $10 per hour? You need money now, right? So do the job, and save that $10 per hour for a course you can use to elevate yourself even higher.

People get paid every day to solve even the smallest problems. Nothing is stopping you from doing the same right now. Want my help? I've got an exercise that'll give you a little push to start building a side income using your everyday in-demand skills.

Exercise: Find Your First Paying Client—or Clients— Before You're Even Done with This Book

Getting started is simple. I want you to reach out to your network through email or on Facebook this week (right now or sometime today if possible!) and offer your help with everyday tasks. Charge a super reasonable $10 to $15 per hour to start. A large percentage of the general population can afford that. It's especially a no-brainer if they can earn more than that $10–$15 per hour in the time you'll save them!

Here's a basic script you can use. Feel free to tweak it as you see fit. Add or remove services you want to promote. Customize it and *go!*

Friends and family in my local area: If you're looking for help around your house or town, I'm available on an hourly basis. I run errands, do laundry, tend to housekeeping chores. I can shop for groceries, organize files or photos, and help with other tasks around your house. My goal is to help you free up extra time in your day so you can enjoy your life more. If you or someone you know could use extra help like this, please let me know.

Add a picture of you smiling if you want to *really* stand out. If you have examples of great organizing projects in your own closet or pantry, post those photos for inspiration. Seeing an example of someone's work has made me hire someone for something I didn't even know I needed *just* because I liked their work so much.

Ask people to share your post with their Facebook friends (make sure the post is set to Public). You could even encourage people to tag friends in your area who might be a fit or know someone who is. As people reach out, offer a rate of $10 or $15 per hour on a trial basis for 30 days or so. Then discuss whether to continue that rate or adjust it.

This type of organic, casual outreach is a solid strategy toward earning some extra dough. Use it to pay off debt, increase cash flow, or put it toward a course or training. Use it to hire a coach or join a community. Any time money is tight, get out and see what you can do to solve a problem for someone else. If you find yourself believing it's too hard or complicated, allow these words haunt you: Making money isn't about you; it's about solving other people's problems. So whose problems can you solve? How? Get creative and have fun with it!

You might not have expected me to push you out of your comfort zone like this, but I hope you'll *do* this assignment and see what happens—even if you're scared. A great way to take the edge off of fear is to "rebrand" your fear into *curiosity*. Get curious about what would happen if you *actually did* this assignment. Putting feelers out to your network might be something you've never, ever done before. But guess what? Doing things you've *never, ever* done before is the first step to getting results you've *never, ever* imagined.

CHAPTER SEVENTEEN
Finding Your Best Long-Term Fit

t's all too easy to get your heart set on doing something to make money because it sounds the easiest or you've got a friend or relative making money doing it. When you see the list of legit ways to work at home, like the one in the next chapter, you might find yourself with a knee-jerk reaction to do *all* the things because doing more means more money faster.

Not so fast! Biting off more than you can chew by trying to do *all* the things is a beeline to burnout and overwhelm. In fact, trying to change your life overnight—or even in a week or two—is why being successful working at home seems so difficult for so many people. They might tell you that they gave up because "it's too hard," but the more likely reality is they didn't give it enough time. I'm sure you've heard the old adage, "Slow and steady wins the race!" There's probably nowhere that adage is more true than here. It's the people who are consistent—and never give up—that win in the long term. Sometimes you have to slow down to speed up, remember!

That list of legit ways to make money from home is coming in Chapter 18, but before we get there I want to make sure you're mentally prepared so you *don't* get overwhelmed. I've got four questions for you to ask yourself. The answers to these questions will make it easier to choose the ideal place to begin your work-at-home journey.

Question No. 1: Which Subject Was Your Favorite in School?

Most of the time I think back to my school days and wonder what the point of 50% of it was. I'm a word nerd, so I *hated* classes like physics, chemistry, and algebra. I knew I'd never do anything with math or science, but I crushed it in English—and any class which required writing.

Looking back, it makes so much sense that I'm doing what I'm doing right now. Words came naturally to me. Friends asked me to proofread their papers so they'd get better grades, get into better schools and—they hoped—make more money. So *technically...* I've been helping people make more money since middle school! It's fun to connect the dots of our past to make sense of our present and empower us to create our future.

What was *your* favorite subject? Did your friends ask you for help on a particular subject? Maybe for you it was English, or maybe it was math, typing, computers, chemistry, or something else entirely. Pretty much any skill you learned in high school can be useful in working at home.

You may decide to start as a tutor. I tutored high school and college students in German before graduating college and earned up to $30 for an hour of my time. I went to their house, but I know many tutors who work out of their homes and even online. Tutoring can grow it into something bigger, like a blog where you sell lesson plans, or you could train other tutors in that subject. The possibilities are endless.

Question No. 2: On a Scale of 1–10, How Detail-Oriented Are You?

You don't *need* to be detail-oriented to make money from home, but you do need to be detail-oriented for *some* types of work. For example, if you're not very detail-oriented, bookkeeping is definitely not the best fit for you. Freelance voice-over work could be a better fit instead. Be honest with yourself about how detail-oriented you are as you consider your options. One of the worst things you can do is choose something that requires you to be *very* detail-oriented... if you're *not* detail-oriented. You'll set yourself up to disappoint your clients.

Question No. 3: Are You a Words or Numbers Person?

Which of the following statements describes you best?

- I love fixing people's writing, and I spot mistakes wherever I go.

- I love writing, helping people write letters, emails, or even telling their stories.

- I love organizing—especially numbers.

- I love watching videos, listening to people speak, and understanding what they have to say.

- I love drinking margaritas while watching *The Jerry Springer Show.*

Pretty much everyone I work with falls into one of the first four categories. They're either good with words, numbers, or creative activities. That's a good thing since there are plenty of work-at-home opportunities for those people.

If you've read this far, you're probably *not* looking to get paid to drink margaritas while watching *Jerry Springer.* That's the way I decided to label the lazy people out there, ha! My point with that is if you don't want to *do* anything and just want to "get money," there's little hope for you. You don't "get" money; you *earn* it.

So which one of the other statements describes you best? Do you geek out about grammar, spelling, and punctuation like I do? Proofreading might be a great option for you. Do you like organizing, adding, subtracting, or otherwise calculating numbers? If so, you might consider helping people as a freelance bookkeeper. You could organize receipts, categorize expenses, or even help prepare their taxes. There are lots of opportunities for people who love numbers—just help people who *hate* numbers!

Do you like creative writing? You can make great money as a freelance writer. My friend Holly is an excellent writer who earns $1 per *word!* Lots of people pay others to write articles, books, or even social media posts. You could also help people turn videos or podcasts into articles for their website.

Maybe you're not a fan of writing, but you enjoy typing. If you can type at least 60 words per minute, look into taking a transcription course to turn your typing skills into a thriving freelance business.

Do you hate words *and* numbers but love creative things? There are plenty of opportunities for you, too! You can use your voice or artistic talents to make money in a myriad of ways.

If none of these get you excited, perhaps you can help bloggers or business owners with day-to-day tasks like responding to blog comments, answering email, or moderating a group. There are literally thousands of ways you can make money. It may take some time to find something that feels right, but you *will* find it! Everybody has their thing.

Question No. 4: How Much Are You Interested in the Business Side of Things?

Does learning business skills that allow you to work from anywhere *excite* you? Are you the type of person who can build a business without someone doing it for you?

Some people aren't interested in building a brand-new business by themselves, and that's totally cool. If that's you, consider freelancing for agencies to start. For example, a writer could be a freelance writer for a ghostwriting agency. You could also do virtual assistant work as part of a virtual assistant agency. You will make a lot less money that way, but it's a great place to start and get valuable experience.

An agency handles all the marketing and business management for you. That's why it's sometimes seen as an advantage to make less money. The agency's cut of your pay goes toward marketing and business management. You just do the work when it comes your way.

Keep in mind that working for an agency doesn't eliminate *all* business issues. You'll still be an independent contractor with tax liability and business expenses to track, but working with an agency that handles marketing means you'll juggle fewer things as a beginner. Win!

Exercise: Write Out Your Answers

Spend some time writing out your answers to these four questions. Grab a sheet of paper and *do it*. Even if it feels weird, redundant, or unnecessary because you have a great memory, do it anyway. Practice taking action. I find taking the little bit of extra time to write out even simple things gives me an extra oomph of inspiration. Something about *seeing it* written down makes a difference!

CHAPTER EIGHTEEN
Your List of Legitimate
Work-At-Home Ideas

Assuming you didn't skip the first part of the book and jump straight to this section, you've got your head on straight in terms of the *mindset* you need to be successful: *Making money is not about you; it's about solving other people's problems.* If that concept sounds foreign to you and you *did* skip straight to this section, go back and read *at least* Part 2. Not kidding. By skipping ahead, you're doing yourself a disservice and may be setting yourself up for failure before you even start! You deserve better than that, so give yourself the gift of doing this the right way. You'll thank *yourself* later!

In this chapter, I'll help you match your interests and abilities to real, legitimate opportunities. There will be no envelope stuffing. There will be no *buying scripts to sell scripts about how to sell scripts…* and you won't end up with a garage full of products.

These opportunities all involve using marketable skills to solve other people's problems. As you read through these, make notes of ones that match your interests and/or current abilities. If you don't have all the skills you need, don't worry; you've got a brain that can *learn!*

At this point, interests and the general abilities are enough to nail down a place to start. So if, for example, you're a grammar nerd but don't know *all* the rules or the mechanics behind proofreading, that's okay. You can learn the rest. If you like technology and podcasts and want to sell podcast editing services, that'll work. You can learn exactly how to do it later. It's not important to see the entire staircase—this is just you taking a single step!

Here are some legitimate opportunities for you to consider. If you want more information about these, visit the Resources page for direct links. On that page, you'll have an opportunity to claim *free lifetime access* to the Work-At-Home Summit. This virtual conference includes 50+ full-length videos featuring experts from all corners of the work-at-home world—including many you'll meet in this chapter!

RESOURCE PAGE (go here and bookmark it if you haven't already!):

WorkAtHomeSchool.com/BookResources

Scoping for Court Reporters

Scoping is another word for *editing* transcripts for court reporters. Editing always happens before proofreading, and it's no different in the world of court reporting. With scoping, you work inside special software to create a cleaner transcript from a court reporter's steno notes. The transcript you edit is then ready for proofreading. Scoping is quite a bit more complicated than proofreading transcripts—so word nerds who learn to scope earn quite a bit more per page than proofreaders. For example, transcript proofreaders earn an average of $0.40 per page; scopists earn $1.00 or more per page. How's that for profitable?!

Now, no one—and I mean *no one*—is naturally good at scoping. Skill and speed come with time and practice. All that work can pay off, though, because scopists can earn up to $60,000 per year! That rivals a court reporter's average earnings. The advantage of scoping versus court reporting is the scopist's ability to work remotely. Court reporters can't report the majority of legal proceedings remotely; they need to be there in the flesh.

For *real* income potential, you could offer scoping *and* proofreading to court reporters. This would make you a valuable asset to reporters in need.

Transcription (General, Legal)

Contrary to what you might've seen online and in TV commercials, transcription work is *real* and *not easy*. You can get jobs with no experience, but you won't get paid very much. Many people have no idea what they're doing and just wing it… and most of those people? They end up giving up after the first two or three jobs because the work is too overwhelming.

I'm a big believer that proper education makes all the difference here. Rushing into something without the proper training is the fastest way to screw it up. Take time to learn, truly hone your skills—and learn how to properly market yourself. If you do that, you're far more likely to find success as a transcriptionist. For example, a trained transcriptionist can earn $1 to $1.50 per minute or more to transcribe important audio or video interviews to text. I work with several such transcriptionists myself! Find legitimate transcription training courses on the Resources page.

Bookkeeping

Did you know you can become a bookkeeper *without* becoming a certified public accountant (CPA)? Yep. They are two different professions, and I personally pay both a CPA and a bookkeeper. The demand is high for skilled bookkeepers, and the demand will keep growing as more and more people build all different types of freelance businesses.

Be careful when signing up for bookkeeping training. You get what you pay for. The only training I recommend is by Ben Robinson. He is a CPA who helps people start a bookkeeping business from home. Ben granted me access to his course, and I was thoroughly impressed. His training can transform you from "a numbers person" to a highly paid bookkeeper in just a few months. Be sure to check out the Resources page for a direct link to Ben's latest training if you want more info about this. The Resources page is at WorkAtHomeSchool.com/BookResources.

You don't have to become a full-fledged bookkeeper, either. You can still earn about $15 per hour cleaning up spreadsheets and making sure the numbers match up.

Virtual Assistance

A virtual assistant (VA) remotely provides services like email management, blog management, tech integration setup, social media scheduling, and so much more! The only limit on what services you can offer as a virtual assistant is what skills you decide to master.

Many of the services listed in this chapter are services that a virtual assistant could do, but I'm listing them separately because specialization is what will set you apart. A Jack/Jill-of-all-trades VA who does a little of everything will earn less than a VA who specializes in two or three high-level skills. An administrative VA will start at between $10-$15 per hour depending on the company, and a more advanced VA can easily charge $20, $30, $40 or more per hour depending on the skill. The market for potential clients is huge, too, because your skills are useful for any type of business in any industry.

The training I recommend for new virtual assistants is *30 Days or Less to Virtual Assistant Success* by Gina Horkey. It's an A-Z roadmap for finding your first client as a VA. You'll get loads of marketing how-to's plus a bunch of software tutorials that will allow you to perform better for your first client. The best part is the super-supportive private Facebook group for students.

Oh, and if you're skeptical that virtual assistants are actually in demand, perhaps this inside look at my business will help. Proofread Anywhere is home to *twelve* virtual assistants who do all kinds of things—even grading exams! Smart bloggers know that they're not just bloggers; they're *online business owners*. If they want to grow, then they need to let go of certain day-to-day tasks (especially email!). Hiring a virtual assistant is one of the wisest moves to make to grow a blog into a thriving online business.

Freelance Writing

Writing is another arena in the work-at-home world where the sky's the limit. *Every* business in *every* niche in *every* part of the world needs quality writing. Scripts, social media posts, proposals, résumés, eBooks, even full-length books… somebody has to write them!

Proofreading skills are a plus if you get into writing so you don't send clients content with typos. It's well worth the investment in proofreading and writing training. You can earn *real* money if your writing quality is high. I know freelance writers who easily earn $100,000 or more each year. They've learned how to position themselves as high-quality providers. I personally pay anywhere from $50 to $500 for blog posts on my site.

Here are training programs you can check out if you're looking to become a freelance writer. You can get an easy list of links to each of these to get more information on the Resources page at WorkAtHomeSchool.com/BookResources.

- **Earn More Writing.** Holly Johnson earns $200,000 per year as a freelance writer. She built that while working full-time in a mortuary, too! The course includes everything she's learned about making serious money writing. It is the most robust course I've found so far to help newbies start a freelance writing career.

- **Start a Résumé-Writing Business.** Everyone who works needs a résumé—especially if they want a job at a desk in the corporate world. Even though it seems like everybody and their mom wants to work at home, thousands of people are still searching for traditional jobs every day! It's a big world out there. If you're great at making people look good on paper, why not get paid for it? Teena Rose, who leads this training, earns $500 to $800 for a résumé and cover letter. Her clients willingly pay this amount for her fabulous work. Teena teaches you how to duplicate *all* her processes in her training. Her course is an excellent value, and it also includes loads of free bonuses.

- **Publish and Sell Your eBooks.** This course puts you inside the publishing industry. It shares tricks of the trade used by traditional publishers to sell lots of books. You'll learn how to target your reading audience and how to get your book distributed around the world—including your local library's virtual shelves.

- **Make Money Writing SEO Articles.** Inkwell Editorial's Yuwanda Black leads this training. She's worked in the freelance writing business since 1993 and has helped thousands of people learn how to write SEO articles and build a clientele—all from home. Get a link to my expert interview with Yuwanda and to her training on the Resources page.

Graphic Design

If you're good with graphics, you can design logos, flyers, ads, or anything else visual for clients. You can work for clients all over the world without leaving your house. Talented designers regularly earn up to $500 per logo.

Answering Phones

Becoming a virtual customer support agent is a good option for beginners. You can earn up to $15 per hour while helping people solve problems via phone. Good support agents can even earn a comfortable full-time income without commuting.

Social Media Management

Social media posting and monitoring takes time. I pay someone $2,000 per month to upload social media posts and monitor comment threads for me. A lot of people do the same as I do. Freelance social media managers can earn between $67,000 to $94,000 per year, depending on their clientele. Even if your only social media skill is Instagram, you can still bring in around $15 per hour.

Audio Editing

I pay a cool guy named Steve to produce my *Work-At-Home Heroes* podcast episodes. For $100 per episode, Steve cleans up my recordings so they're ready for publication. He's a saint, too, because sometimes I am a *sloppy* interviewer... but when you listen to the finished product, you can't tell!

Proofreading

One of my former proofreading students tagged me on Instagram in a photo with an inspiring caption that read, "Doing what I could have never done before! Working from my balcony while on vacation in Prague! Thank you, Caitlin, for this opportunity!"

Proofreading is one of my *favorite* work-from-anywhere options, of course! This *one skill* paid the bills after I got fired. It paved the way for me to start my blog and write this book. It helped Katie, who wrote the foreword for this book, snowball her way to a massively rewarding career as a work-at-home project manager.

With the explosion of self-publishing, online businesses, and blogging, the demand for proofreading is not only high, it's increasing rapidly. Proofreaders can earn up to $60 per hour depending on the text. If you're a word nerd with an affinity for finding errors, head over to ProofreadAnywhere.com to learn more.

Editing Books and Web Content

You can carve out a niche editing books for first-time authors and earn $0.05 or more per word. Depending on the length of the book, this could add up to hundreds or even thousands of dollars per book. Choose a type of book you love, and start getting paid to edit books you'd normally pay to read. Sounds like a win to me!

Freelance Marketing Strategist or Consultant

Do you have a background (education or experience) in marketing? If so, you can earn $100 or more per hour as a freelance marketing strategist or consultant.

Voice-over Acting

Is your voice *made* for radio? If so, you can make $72 per hour or more talking into a computer-connected microphone while sitting at home. As you gain experience, your rate can increase significantly from there.

Photography

Even a "side hobby" business of photography can bring in $2,000 or more per weekend for wedding photography. You can get started with newborn photography, sports photography, family photography, and dozens of other types. While the shooting can't be done at home (unless you have a portrait studio at home!), the editing is done at home. Not keen on shooting photos but know your way around Photoshop? Network with local photographers to sniff out opportunities to edit their photos. I'm friends with several photographers here in Central Florida who pay remote editors.

Odd Jobs

What tasks do you enjoy doing around the house or neighborhood? Market doing those tasks to people who don't like to do it or who want to "buy time" as I do. You can run errands, do laundry, clean houses, or mow lawns. You can put out and collect signs for real estate agents. You can even drive people to appointments or sell their stuff on craigslist for a cut of the profit.

> **BONUS**
> Visit the Resources page at WorkAtHomeSchool.com/BookResources for a printable list of 73 skills and services you could potentially offer to make money at home.

Exercise: Explore the List... But Don't Let it Limit You

The good news? What I can fit into this chapter *doesn't even scratch the surface* of all possible work-at-home ideas. You can make money doing almost anything, and sometimes the best place to start is so obvious you could easily miss it. That was me with proofreading. If I had known how in-demand proofreading was when I got fired, I probably never would've enrolled in personal training school—and I would've built my freelance proofreading business to $40,000+ per year a lot sooner!

Spend a few minutes jotting down notes on the things that jumped out at you in this chapter and/or the bonus list from the Resources page. What do you *not* want to do? What ideas lit you up as you were reading about them? Write that stuff down.

In the next chapter, I'll help you identify the right opportunity for you. Let's go!

CHAPTER NINETEEN
Identifying Your Top 5
Best Options to Consider

B efore I launched Work-At-Home School, I committed to making it the most robust resource on working at home. Work-At-Home School needed to include *everything*— mindset, time management, self-care, and plenty of skills training. To make sure I didn't miss anything, I asked my Facebook network what their #1 frustration or concern was with working at home.

I was pleasantly surprised by how many people responded to my post. Two comments stuck out above the rest. One person worried they'd waste time and money learning a skill and not end up using that skill over the long term. Why? Because they'd find out it wasn't their passion. They were afraid to do anything until they "found their passion."

The second comment that stuck out was from someone worried they wouldn't be able to find the perfect side gig. The idea they'd make the wrong choice from all the options had them frozen—

afraid to do *anything* until they were confident they found their "perfect side gig."

These concerns are common, and I hear variations of them on a daily basis. The pursuit of passion or perfection before starting *something* is often a gigantic stumbling block toward success. If I waited for this book to be "perfect" in my eyes before publishing it, it never would've been published at all. If you're waiting for the perfect opportunity—or the perfect time—you'll be waiting forever. So forget about "perfect" and take a step *today* using what you know *now.*

Being passionate about what you do is important. That's why it's one part of my four-part test for finding a good fit for you. But—big but!—passion isn't necessary to get started. You likely won't experience a crazy epiphany or have a dream that reveals your true passion. So how do you find your passion? Well, for many of us, the best way to find it is to *take action.* You'll figure it out as you go.

Chances are, your first work-at-home job won't be what you do the rest of your life. That's totally okay—it wasn't for me, either. Proofreading originally served to fill in the income gaps after getting fired. When I started helping people make money proofreading through my blog, I thought *that* was my passion. As I helped more people, though, I realized my true passion wasn't helping people with proofreading specifically; it was helping them develop and market *skills.* If I'd never started proofreading simply because it wasn't my passion, I might've never discovered my *real* passion.

So if you're just getting started, forget about your passion for now. Just start doing *something.* Remember the saying that you have to "kiss a few frogs to find a prince"? Well, it's true in business, too.

You'll likely find a bunch of things you don't want to do—but those things *aren't* a waste of time. They're stepping stones toward that thing you love so much you'd do it for free.

It's *very* rare to find the thing you love immediately. Take it from me, a work-at-home teacher who once shelled out $7,000 for personal training school only to quit after three years. Better yet, ask 10 college grads over 40 years old if their degree relates to what they're doing now. Almost nobody ends up on the same career path they start out on, but the most successful people make the best decisions they can and just pivot as they go. If you invest time and money into something and realize you don't enjoy it as much as you thought you would, then quit. Learn from it and move on.

Now is a good time to differentiate between quitting and giving up. They aren't the same thing. *Quitting* means you've realized something just isn't worth it to you anymore; *giving up* means you decided you couldn't do it. You *quit* a job because you don't need the money. You *give up* trying to work at home because "it's too much work" or you'll "probably fail anyway." See the difference? Quitting is totally fine if it means you're *not* giving up on your goal. Life is simply too short to keep doing something you don't like. It's too short to be mad at yourself for "wasting time" on something you don't enjoy. When you're learning, no time is ever wasted.

Imagine if you had started this journey two, three, or even five years ago. You probably would've made—and learned from—a *bunch* of mistakes by now. Mistakes are never reasons to give up. Sometimes they're reasons to pivot, but they're never reasons to give up. When I realized I didn't want to be a personal trainer, I lost a lot of sleep over it. I *hated* pivoting away from something into which I'd invested a lot of time and money. I beat myself up for a while, but then I got over it because I moved on to something better.

There's so much value in being open to new things. When I started proofreading, I never imagined I'd be training thousands of people online to do the same thing. I just rolled with what came naturally to me. When new opportunities came my way, I didn't refuse to do anything else because I was already established as a proofreader; I kept my mind open. I took action to learn new things and slowly, my knack for proofreading evolved into a true passion for helping people make money at home.

That's the beauty of the work-at-home world. You're in charge, and nothing has to be permanent. Keep your mind open as you take action, and you may find things you never knew existed that you *love* to do.

Exercise: Generate a "Top 5" List of Ideas

We all start somewhere. I started with proofreading. For this exercise, grab a fresh sheet of paper and list your top five ideas. Make sure they're things you can see yourself doing that help other people. Leave other people's opinions out of it for now; this is about you. Work off of the last chapter's exercise as a foundation for choosing your top five ideas.

Don't worry about which one to try first or the specifics of how you'll make money from those ideas yet—that comes later. The point of this exercise is to take the pressure of finding the "one" perfect idea off your shoulders. That's why I want you to pick at least five ideas. It's also designed to free your mind from the pressure of finding your one true passion. The word alone puts so much pressure on people who are just getting started. My advice? *Fuggedaboutit.* For now, anyway.

CHAPTER TWENTY
Filtering Your Top 5 Ideas

How exciting! You've created a list of skills you can use to make money at home. The most popular reason I hear from folks in the Work-At-Home Heroes group on Facebook for why they haven't yet taken action is *not knowing where to start*… yet here you are with a list of five potential starting points! That puts you *way* ahead of the curve. Nice work!

In this chapter, you'll filter those top five ideas down to *one* thing to start with that you believe could be a solid long-term fit for you. If you pursue that idea and it's not the right fit, that's okay—just choose something else from your list.

Don't fret if you don't yet have the skills to pursue the idea you choose right now. You can learn the skills, and you don't have to break the bank to do that. It's next to impossible to make good money in the long term without training and practice, but that doesn't mean you can't get started by learning very basic skills and earning entry-level income from it. Set aside some of your "beginner bucks" to invest in further training later.

Knowing that additional training is necessary to grow your income makes some people sad. If that's you, I invite you to read through the chapters about the lies and myths that hold people back. Perhaps you've been battling with the fixed mindset that nothing will ever change for you; that you've been dealt a sorry hand in life. Consider everything that exists outside of what you know. What you *believe* is possible for you is often very different from what is *actually* possible for you. So I also invite you to keep your mind open. *Learning changes everything.* What you put into your brain directly affects what comes out of it!

Reprogramming your mind to believe you can achieve just about anything gets people excited, but that excitement by itself isn't what gets the cash rolling in. Taking action to solve problems is what will make you money. Never, *ever* lose sight of that. As long as there are problems in the world, there will be endless opportunities for action takers to make money.

My job is to help you combine your knowledge and actions so you can generate *real* income. You'll have everything you need to get started with the 28-day launch plan in Chapter 22, but first we need to whittle down your five ideas to just one—and any good option *must* pass the four-part test. Let's take a closer look at each part of that test so you can make sure your idea checks all the boxes as an ideal starting point.

Filtering Your Options Through the 4-Part Test

I won't perpetuate the widespread myth that it's *easy* to make a solid income working from home... because it's not! The higher paying the job, the bigger problems you'll need to learn to solve. If you expect to make even just an extra $10,000 or so a year without putting in any effort, then you're not looking for *work* at home; you're looking for free money... and there's no such thing!

It's worth the work. *You're* worth the work. Take one step at a time as you build your business. Right now, that step is to narrow down your list of ideas from five to one using the four-part test. We'll be bringing passion back in a bit, too, and now's as good a time as any to remind you *not* to let "finding your passion" stall you out! You don't need passion to start—and passion is almost *never* the result of time wasted in the endless vortex of research.

For now, list each of your five ideas on its own sheet of paper. Then walk through the four-part test for each of them. If you're unsure, study what other people are doing, make your best educated guess, and move on. The goal here isn't to be perfect; it's just to filter your list down to a starting point for you. If you get through the exercise and you still have more than one, that's okay. You'll be down to one skill to market by the time we get to the 28-day launch plan in Chapter 22.

Part 1: It must not be a scam.

You learned how to smell scams in Chapter 14, so you're probably in good shape here, but make sure your list only includes *legitimate* ideas. A good question to ask is if the work you'd perform would help people… or just allow you to "get money." Remove anything like envelope stuffing or home typing. Do you have to pay money to get started? If so, what are you paying for? Are you paying money to get equipment—like an iPad or a laptop—to help you do the work? Are you buying a bunch of products to resell? Some upfront expenditures are okay, but just make sure you know what they are.

Make a note of what you already have and what you think you'd need to buy to get into each business. Don't worry about knowing *everything* about an idea at this point. Just identify possible scams. Look for warning signs such as having to recruit others, buy a "starter kit," or fill your garage with inventory. That's much different than needing a computer, printer, or iPad to do the work.

Part 2: It must be predictably profitable.

I know this one seems obvious. While oodles of well-meaning people start businesses from home that *seem* profitable on the surface, not all businesses are *actually* profitable when you factor in how long it takes to do the work. Folks who are not good at typing, for example, could make less per hour as a transcriptionist than I made as a cashier at Winn-Dixie! Other folks seem to make a profit, but it's not as much as expected after factoring in time and other expenses.

A good example of this is driving with one of the ride-sharing apps. Companies advertise that you can make hundreds of dollars per week driving a car you already own. While that's true, consider the cost of gas, repairs, wear and tear on your car, and downtime between rides. You only make money when someone's in your car.

Include those variables when calculating how much money you're actually making for your time.

To be *truly* profitable, your business needs to be actually worth your *time!* One good way to figure out if something's profitable is to learn from others. If someone else is earning a solid income doing what you want to do, that's a good sign. Of course, it's hard to know if someone is *truly* making money, but many great, growth-minded people share how much they make, like I did with proofreading. If you're considering enrolling in a skill-building course, look for instructors with a *lot* of student case studies and success stories. The more, the better—that kind of stuff should confirm whether or not the skill is something *you* could offer to earn money as well.

It's common to assume that because a bunch of people are doing what you want to do that the market is *saturated.* If you're battling that assumption right now, take a deep breath. Go ahead—inhale. Now exhale. The market isn't saturated, and it never will be. The internet is an ever-expanding universe. If lots of other people are freelancing with the skill you want to turn into a business, that means there is real demand. If you have a valuable skill and the ability to market it, there is plenty of opportunity for you.

It's not easy to work at home, and not everyone who attempts to make it work will have the guts to keep going when things get tough. I like to look at that as a process of natural selection in the work-at-home world. *Only the strong survive.* That means the lazy people, the ones who just want free money, and the ones who are unwilling to stop thinking about themselves probably won't make it very far—leaving even more room for you to make your mark... and your money.

Part 3: It must fit your personality.

Lean in on this one. Making real money with a skill requires hard work and a never-give-up attitude. So you need to consider a few things. What will it actually take for you to do the hard work associated with your idea? Will you enjoy it? Enjoying it, for the record, doesn't mean every minute includes puppies and rainbows. You just don't want to create a job you hate. For example, if you hate reading but love watching videos, proofreading is probably not the best fit for you, but editing videos could be fantastic.

Another consideration is how important it is for you to be location independent. Some people, like me, despise the thought of needing to be in a specific place at a certain time to work. That's why teaching classes at the gym didn't work out for me. Other people *love* having a designated place and time for work. If you have a preference, go through your list and see which ideas fit your preference best. If you're unsure if one of the skills you listed requires you to be somewhere (even home), just put a note that you're unsure. You might not know this information for a while, and that's okay.

You might find unexpected ways to make things location independent. For example, if you need to store and ship physical products, you're not location independent—but you might be able to *drop ship* physical products. With drop shipping, all you need is to process the order. That process is often totally automated. Once the order processes, someone else then ships the product from *their* inventory. You can do this from a computer anywhere in the world.

Doing people's laundry or walking people's dogs is difficult to do from any location. You could build a team of others that you manage remotely, but you'll have to do most of the work yourself initially. Keep those things in mind as you consider your ideas. If you want *true* work freedom, narrow down your list to things you can do from *anywhere* using just a computer or phone.

Identify which of the skills you identified have repeat clients. That will make it so you don't have to market constantly. Résumé writing is a legitimate work-from-anywhere job… but most people don't need résumés more than once a year or so. You'd need to market all the time to keep things going. There's nothing *wrong* with that, and I know people who make good money writing résumés. Just consider the extra time it'll take to establish yourself and keep your income stable.

Skills with repeat clients include proofreading, transcribing, writing, laundry, and virtual assistance. Those are services people need over and over again. You could fill a full-time income by getting even five or 10 clients with some skills. Which of your skills are in industries with repeat clients?

Part 4: It must fit your passion.

Be careful here. Hardly anybody new to the work-at-home world *truly* knows which business fits their passion. Even people who've been playing the game for years don't know what their passion is yet. I include passion in the four-part test anyway, though, because it's important to have in the back of your mind over the long term. *You don't need passion to start.*

For now, all I want you to do is ask yourself specifically how each skill on your list helps people. Why is it important? How would it make you feel to solve a problem using that skill? What kind of problems could you solve?

Remember how I told you I wasn't all that passionate about proofreading? At first, I did it because I was good at it and could make money. But when I started proofreading transcripts, the passion started to develop. I still wouldn't call it passion, but there was a spark (or something). I was hooked on finding errors and polishing my clients' product—and the better I got with technology, the more money I could make, so that was a bonus, too. Even though it wasn't my passion, proofreading transcripts was still my primary source of income for three years in a row.

So again: *You don't need passion to start.* It can come later and, often, after a pivot or two. Sometimes the skill isn't what you're passionate about, either; it's the people you serve with that skill. You can't know any of that unless you get started with something. I had no idea how great it would feel to help court reporters. I just knew I liked catching typos and that people would pay me for it.

For now, that's all I want *you* to do with each skill on your list. Ask whether you like *doing* the work and what impact you could make by helping people that way. If you don't have the skill yet, look for other people doing it and ask yourself if you think you'd like doing the work. Feel free to reach out and ask them what they love about their work, too—if they gush about it, that's a good sign! Remember, we're just narrowing things down, and none of this is set in stone. It's okay and even encouraged to make adjustments along the way.

Exercise: Rewrite Your List of Ideas

After going through the four-part test above, did any skills rise up as better options than others? Did any drop off completely?

Do you have open questions? Are you unsure about whether something can be truly location independent or profitable? If so, do some research now to see what you can find out about your open questions. Just beware the endless vortex!

At this point, you should be close to having just one skill that stands out above the rest of your top five. If you're having trouble deciding between two or three, hop over to the Work-At-Home Heroes group on Facebook and poll the group for their opinion. Sometimes letting your peers in on your decision making reveals blind spots in your process—and you always get *super* valuable insight!

CHAPTER TWENTY-ONE
Setting Yourself Up for
Your 28-Day Launch

Beffore you get started on the 28-day launch plan, I want to remind you that it takes *work* to make money. Some people who started reading this book will never make it to this chapter because the idea of actually *working* to earn more money turns them off—and that's why I believe there will always be endless opportunities for people who *do* want to work.

The sad truth is that for many people, it's not the actual work that turns them off. The deeper reason they don't start is because they don't believe they have what it takes to *do* the work. It's an internal block—it's *not* that the work is impossibly hard. We doubt not the opportunity in front of us but *ourselves* and our ability to learn and solve problems. That belief causes us to sabotage ourselves. We're our own worst enemies. The work isn't difficult—*we* are difficult.

Your ability to make money is a result of 1) the choices you make and 2) the actions you take. This book isn't magical; I'm not magical. I'm a Hogwarts reject, remember? You might be a reject too, but that doesn't mean you don't have any power. In fact, you have *all* the power. You know the cheesy saying, "If it's to be, then it's up to me"? Allow that to empower you, not overwhelm you. Don't get caught up in the endless vortex of research trying to see the entire staircase before you take the first step. For many of us, the staircase isn't even there yet because you'll be building it yourself— one step at a time.

If you wake up every morning thinking you have no control over your life, that belief will hold you captive. If you don't believe any of your choices will make a difference, it's a lot harder to take action for positive change—and it's far easier to blame someone or something else for your lack of results. Stuck in place, spinning your wheels, you'll make the same choices, take the same actions, and get the same results. On the other hand, if you wake up each day knowing that each choice *does* matter, the tables turn. You're empowered to succeed. This isn't some hippie nonsense... *mindset is everything.*

A lot of us grew up believing that people who earned a lot of money were cheating somehow. I grew up with that belief. Even after I started making honest money online, I still felt like *I* was cheating somehow! It didn't matter how many people wrote to me about how much money they made because of my training; I felt like a fraud. Sometimes I still do.

What's the secret to succeeding anyway even if you feel like the authorities may show up at any time to shut you down? You must keep moving. Just because you *feel* like you have no business trying to increase your income doesn't mean you don't have all the power to do it. Just because you *feel* like you can't learn any new skills doesn't mean you can't. Just because you *believe* something is true doesn't mean it *is* true. In the case of self-doubt, it's almost always *not* true.

Another limiting belief I struggled with was that having a business meant signing up for an endless battle to survive. I thought my business would actually own me. I believed that based on words of warning from well-meaning relatives—and because I saw my family's business flourish and then ultimately fail. I don't think it *had* to fail, but it did. We blamed the economy at the time, but knowing what I know now, the economy wasn't to blame; we were. We didn't evolve our brick-and-mortar business to the online world, and *that* was what hurt us in the end. None of us knew how to use the internet to make money... but our competitors did.

If we'd learned how to leverage the internet to make money, I'm *positive* the business would still be thriving. If we continued to hone our skills to be cutting-edge in our market, we'd continue to thrive... but we didn't. Because we didn't continue to invest in the skills we needed to thrive, the business couldn't survive.

Watching my family's business fail taught me even more hard truths about "making it" in today's online world:

1) It's not a problem with the economy.

2) It's not a problem with where you live.

3) It's not even a problem with the degree you got or didn't get in college. It's a problem with your *skills*.

It's just a matter of *knowing how to do stuff*... then taking action on it.

Except... we don't like to admit *we don't know* what we're doing. We don't like to admit we need help—especially those of us with college degrees or previous business experience. Ironically, "I don't know how" is often the reason we give for not doing the stuff we dream of doing! I put off starting my blog for pretty much *forever* because I didn't know how to get a website up and running. If I could go back in time, I'd slap myself across the face and say, "Google it, you big sissy!"

Fortunately for you, you're not a big sissy—and thanks to all the mistakes I've made in building my businesses, you'll spend far less time googling stuff than I did!

Final Words on Identifying Your Best Options

At this point, the only thing stopping you from getting started is you. Start with the 28-day launch plan in the next chapter. The steps are broken down enough that it shouldn't overwhelm you, but even if it scares you, *do the things*. The only way to build confidence in anything is to do more of it.

You're ready; you're not alone; and you're closer to success than you think. If you've done all the exercises so far and follow the 28-day launch plan, you may very well find yourself earning extra money by this time next month—possibly even sooner!

For more help and support as you get started:

- Visit the Resources page at WorkAtHomeSchool.com/ BookResources where you'll find *oodles* (I love that word) of high-value resources—including lifetime access to the Work-At-Home Summit online conference (a $297 value).

- Join tens of thousands of other growth-oriented individuals in the Work-At-Home Heroes group on Facebook.

- Consider enrolling in Work-At-Home School for a complete, insanely high-value way to fast-track your skill building and income.

Email me directly with any questions! caitlin@ workathomeschool.com

PART TWO
(continued)

Step 3:
Launch

CHAPTER TWENTY-TWO
Your 28-Day Launch

W ant to know the *real* secret to success? Success boils down to a simple multiplication equation containing two variables: skills and action.

$$SKILLS \times ACTION = SUCCESS$$

It's just math. If your skills are at a zero and you take zero action, you'll get zero success. Logically. Say you have a low number like "1" for skills, yet you take a *ton* of action with that skill. You'll have far more success than someone who has ton of skills but takes zero action.

That's all there is to it. Plain, simple, and refreshingly realistic, huh? No gimmicks, false promises, schemes, or scams. What you can get on the right side of the equation is without limit because you have total control over the variables on the left side.

The success equation works *all* the time. Yes; you'll sometimes deal with external variables beyond your control that can affect the outcome, but both variables in this equation are largely controlled by *you*. Own it. Don't allow excuses like "I need more skills" to keep you from taking action. Even if you're still saving for the training you want, you can still manipulate the other variable in the equation: action. Take action with the skill(s) you have and watch what happens to the right side!

You've already identified your current skills—and you already started taking action with the short brainstorming and filtering assignments at the end of the most recent chapters. You've got momentum; now it's time to ramp it up. To help you do that, I designed this 28-day launch plan.

The more time you're able to dedicate to each day's activity, the quicker you'll start earning money. If you only have two hours per *week*, your business will take longer to build than someone who has two hours per *day*. Even with two hours per day, it's still possible— as long as you take *consistent* action in the time you have. Slow and steady still yields results.

This blueprint works best for people willing to dedicate at least two focused hours a day to their business. However, if you have more time and energy, feel free to move forward at any pace that works for you! It's broken down into three phases, each lasting 8-10 days. The first phase is when you'll get "ready" to launch. Yes, "ready" is in quotes because ready—without quotes—is a myth. If you wait until you feel ready, you'll never start. The second phase is where you get "set." On those days, you'll set yourself up with the basics of building and marketing your skills. In the final phase, you "go." This is where you take the action that will develop your confidence.

I've also put a digital workbook version of this launch plan on the Resources page. Visit WorkAtHomeSchool.com/BookResources to download it!

Here we go!

Day 1: Write your goals.

Before you can get where you want to go, you need to know where you're heading. Do you like your job but want to earn an extra $100, $500, or $1,000 a month? Do you hate your job or hate your career path and want to replace your entire income? Do you want to move? Do you want to pay off your debt?

Grab a piece of paper and write out everything you *want*. Although this is a 28-day blueprint to going from an idea to income, think more than 28 days away. Start by writing, "One year from now, I will..." at the top of the piece of paper. Below it, list all the things you want. The sky's the limit, and don't worry about being perfect. Just get started. You can adjust as you go.

Over the next 10 days, I'm going to help you get "ready" to create income all on your own. Remember why "ready" is in quotes. Way too many people wait until they *feel* ready to start. Months or even years later, they still don't feel ready. Don't let the way you *feel* dictate what you *do*. There will always be more you can learn about business and marketing; you can always improve your skill over time. You can learn as you go... and the time to go is now!

Put it this way: For the rest of these first 10 days, you're going to get ready *enough* to get started.

Day 2: What would it mean to you to accomplish that goal?

Go back through your goals from Day 1. What would your life be like if that all came to fruition? Today I want you to describe your ideal life in vivid detail. Dream big. Dig deep on your "why." When you keep the reasons for your goals at the front of your mind, moving forward takes far less effort.

Day 3: Pinpoint your skills.

By now, you know you can make money doing almost anything. For today, just spend a few minutes identifying the skills you'll look into. Do you like to read? Do you have a great radio voice? Are you good at proofreading? Do you like to sew? Can you draw well? Are you talented in graphic design? Write down as many skills as you can. Nothing is too small.

If you need a boost of inspiration, sign up for free access to the Work-At-Home Summit via the Resources page. Watch a few videos on topics that pique your interest. If you've already pinpointed your skills, move on to Day 4!

RESOURCE PAGE

FREE Lifetime Access to the Work-At-Home Summit: Visit WorkAtHomeSchool.com/ BookResources to claim yours.

Day 4: Who is making money selling those skills?

Choose a favorite from your list of skills. You may have already done this in Chapter 20. If you've still got two or more, choose just one that you love doing, are already great at, and would enjoy developing further. Your task today is to look for other people who are already making money selling those skills.

First, look for people who are only a *few* steps ahead of you who are selling services but don't have huge audiences. This will give you some ideas for making money with your skills in the short-term. You may want to try a search inside the Work-At-Home Heroes Facebook group—it's quite likely there are some folks a few steps ahead of you right inside this community! Remember *not* to let yourself get turned off by seeing other people making money doing your thing. Competition is merely proof that the skill is in-demand and that people have no problem paying for it.

Second, look for people who are the best of the best. Who is the *top dog* in your industry that everyone models themselves after? What do they sell? How do they sell it? This will give you some ideas for making money with your skills over the longer term. A little warning here, too—it can be common to see the top dogs and think, "I'll *never* be at that level!" But the top dogs were all puppies once upon a time… *every* expert was once a beginner!

If you don't like what you see from your first choice, go through the same process for other skills you've identified. Find one you're excited about over the short and long term.

For example, if you have a great radio voice, look for people who use their voice to make money. (Hint: There are a few Work-

At-Home Heroes podcast episodes on this topic!) You might find people a few steps ahead of you doing voice-over work for short videos and podcast intros. You might also find more seasoned voice-over artists who voice commercials and audiobooks. If that work excites you, becoming a voice-over artist may be a good choice.

Day 5: How much do others charge?

Go through your list of people making money using skills that you have. How much do they charge for those services? Many freelancers have rates on their website. You can also get standard rate information from industry associations or publications. For example, you can find freelance writing rates in a book called *Writer's Market*. Similarly, the Editorial Freelancers Association lists standard editing rates on their site. You can find a link to their site on the Resources page.

Keep in mind that the amount you can earn depends on several factors. Rates tend to increase along with your skill and experience level. You might start out earning *less* than standard rates until you've improved your skills and built a portfolio of references. So take all rate information as informational only. Published rate information can also help you break a tie between two skills. If you dig the idea of two skills, you might as well start with the one that'll earn you the most money.

Here I go with another warning. Once you get your baseline details on what other folks are up to, *shut it down.* Watching other people incessantly often has the same effect as the endless vortex of research. It can cost you a *lot* of time spent worrying and fighting the urge to copy everything someone else does. Personally, I ignore pretty much everyone most of the time. I don't get caught up in what so-and-so is doing, and I never base my potential for success on someone else's results. My success depends entirely on *my* actions—as does yours.

Day 6: Where can you develop your skills?

Over the first five days, you set goals, listed skills, and researched people making money using those skills. Today I want you to look for places you can continue to develop each of the skills you've researched. For example, if you're a word nerd like me, proofreading might be a good fit. Look for places you can learn about proofreading (the Resources page has some excellent ideas).

The goal is to enable yourself to constantly improve your skills. The lifelong learning component is critical because the better you get, the more you can charge! Watch out for limiting beliefs here. You *can* find places to develop your skills that don't break the bank. You do *not* need to go back to college for an expensive degree.

If you're just getting started and don't yet have a skill you need, don't freak out. You can learn it. Your brain has an infinite capacity, so get excited about what doors will open for you when you fill it with new things. Remember Stephanie Spillmann from HealthySavvyAndWise.com? We talked about her in the "Warning" section at the beginning of this book. She wasn't very tech-savvy when she started, but that didn't keep her from becoming a professional proofreader and blogger. She was super scared at first—she had no website or marketing skills and was totally green to online business. But she found help, built her staircase to success one step at a time, and has continued to learn every day since. There are plenty of places to learn online without having to go back to college. Visit the Resources page for a bunch of them!

Day 7: Where can you get business skills?

Providing a service is one thing, but marketing that skill—the actual business part—is another big piece of the pie. Good news, though: You don't need to have a business degree to run a business. Yay!

Today, look for places where you can get some business support or direction. Make sure these places include information about turning the skill into a business. Do you get access to a support community of others building similar businesses? You might find these things in the very same place you develop your skills. With Proofread Anywhere's courses, I include two whole modules on how to turn your skills into a business.

In Work-At-Home School, you get access to several skill-building courses plus dozens of full-length resources on goal-setting, mindset, and overcoming fear and money mental blocks. You develop marketable skills you can use to grow your income. You'll get and *stay* organized so you can be productive, happy, and healthy in business. Many programs can teach skills, but very few provide supporting content for *everything else* you'll face as you write your own income story.

Check out the Resources page for other courses I recommend.

Day 8: Where can you get support?

Working from home is not easy, but if you have strong support from like-minded people, you can save yourself a lot of time and keep yourself focused. The best support system is one that encourages you *and* keeps you accountable.

If you don't have support around you, find it online. Most quality skills courses have a community component to them, but if you're just getting your feet wet, take advantage of the free Work-At-Home Heroes community on Facebook. There are tons of free resources inside, including Q&A videos, eBooks, and podcast episodes.

Strong support also helps you make better decisions and take the emotions out of issues. Knowing you're not in this alone can literally make the difference between giving up and pushing forward.

Day 9: Commit to investing in yourself like a business—because you are your business!

If you want people to take you seriously, you need to take *yourself* seriously. You've just spent an entire week planning your business. You set a goal. You identified skills that others use to make money and that interest you. You found places to improve your skills and build your business chops. You've taken action. You've begun to build your staircase. That's something many people want yet never do... and here you are, *doing it.* So believe in yourself. Respect the work you've put in. Take your new business seriously.

Focus and continued action will help you get the most return on your investment. Sign up for one skill-learning course, one business-learning course, and one community. If you don't know where to start or you're strapped for cash you need to invest in high-quality training, check out the Resources page to register for free access to the Work-At-Home Summit that is brimming with ideas and helpful tools.

Day 10: Identify the time you will commit to building your business.

How much time will you spend on your business? What days? What hours? Grab a calendar or go to your online calendar and block that time out. Commit to using that time for your business.

Remember, this needs to work with your life situation. If you work 80 hours a week at a day job, you can't put in as much time as someone only working part-time. If you're a single parent of three toddlers, you won't be able to dedicate as much time as someone without kids. Even if you've got just one hour a day, you can still do this. I've seen all kinds of people in some downright crazy situations make it happen. *It's all a choice.* Choose the time each day you'll dedicate to building your business, and choose stick to it.

Day 11: Determine how you'll position your service and to whom you'll market it.

Today, decide what you will sell, and write a short sentence describing what you offer, to whom, and why. Keep it simple yet specific.

Here's a simple fill-in-the-blank template you can use to write your description. The fancy name for this description of what you offer is *Unique Selling Proposition,* or USP.

I help _____ do _____ so
they can _____ .

Say you want to be a virtual assistant for health bloggers. "I'm a VA for health bloggers" is simple, but it's not specific. *This* is specific: "I help health bloggers simplify their inbox and social media scheduling so they can have more time to create useful content for their audience."

What's cool about developing a USP is that it doubles as the opening of your "elevator pitch." If you're attending a health blogger conference to network with new potential clients and someone asks you what you do, opening with this line is clear and concise. You want this description to incite a response from your ideal client such as, "Wow; *I need that.*"

A clear statement of exactly what you do, for whom, and why should put *them* at the center because... drumroll, please: *Making money is not about you.* Never, ever forget that. So your description should never be you-centered. Let me morph the last example into a bad one. "I do inbox and social media management for health bloggers so I can make money and have more time with my kids." Which one would make someone more inclined to hire you? Which one would make *you* want to hire you?

If you're clear on *who* your ideal client is, but you're not sure *what* you could do to help them, I outlined a very simple strategy in Chapter 11 to help you figure it out. The strategy features a 100%

success rate, and it's just a single word: ASK. Go to a conference to network, email your favorite health bloggers, ask a question in a relevant online forum... *ask* what issues your ideal client faces in their business each day.

You'll likely hear the same things over and over, but occasionally you'll land on someone with a unique problem. Maybe they get to Inbox Zero every day and have their social media down pat but struggle when it comes to keeping up with blog comments or graphic design. This strategy is also an excellent way to whittle down your list of skills *and* get new ideas for which skills to build next as you increase your income. Use the magic of asking to figure out what problems your ideal client has and *learn to solve them.*

I've got more good news for you. Once you've created your simple description, you also have an attention-grabbing headline for your website and social media profiles. Your website should make it easy to determine what you do, for whom, and why. Your unique selling proposition does exactly that. You might be tempted to leave out the "why," but *don't* leave it out. The more you can speak to *why* they want to work with you—what *they* get out of it—the more likely you are to draw them in.

Day 12: Decide your pricing.

Decide what you'll charge for your services. Revisit the research you did on Day 5, and type out your own list of services and accompanying rates. Some freelancers create a printable PDF brochure or sheet containing descriptions of all their services and their rates so it's easier to provide this information to prospective clients via email and on LinkedIn.

Day 13: Identify 10 potential clients or customers.

Today, start looking for clients in your current network. Who is a good prospect for your business? Once you've exhausted your current network, look local to your neighborhood.

Suppose you wanted to write blog posts for salon owners to help them attract more customers. Google for salons in your area and record their contact information in a spreadsheet. (Grab a free template for this on the Resources page!) Do you know any salon owners or people who work in salons? Record those names down as well. Don't worry about next steps yet; you're just building a list of potential clients right now. Soon, your task will be to contact those potential clients.

Day 14: Identify 10 influencers and/or peers.

Yesterday, you began creating a list of potential clients. Today, you'll identify people who could *influence* your customers or clients to work with you.

To continue the salon example, look for people who either work with or create content for salon owners. For example, you might identify web designers, graphic designers, social media agencies, podcasters, or writers who have clients in the salon or beauty industries. It's important that you don't limit your network to potential clients. Establishing relationships with other service providers can easily earn you referrals. Even if they provide the same service, they're still a valuable contact. I remember when I got too busy as a proofreader, I'd refer my clients to trustworthy peers they could trust.

The closer your relationship with these people, the better. The closer you are with them, the more likely they are to refer business your way. Getting introductions from influencers and peers is helpful because there's automatically a level of trust there. I'm much more likely to hire someone based on a glowing recommendation from a friend than I am to just hire someone randomly.

Inside the Work-At-Home Summit, you'll find a few videos with even more ideas to connect with influencers. Visit WorkAtHomeSchool.com/BookResources to get free lifetime access.

Day 15: Update your social media profiles.

Does your LinkedIn profile have a professional picture and job history? How about that new USP you developed on Day 11? Update your profile so it looks professional and includes your new business. Write in the present tense, as if you are already in business (because you are, even if you haven't sold anything yet). Include all the services you offer plus any relevant courses and other training you've taken. If you've done any work for friends or family, ask them to leave an endorsement on your profile.

For example, let's assume you want to pursue transcript proofreading. If you completed my *Transcript Proofreading: Theory and Practice*™ course, list it by name and the skills you learned from it. Training shows potential clients you're serious and invested in providing them with the highest level of service possible.

Once you're done with LinkedIn, update your profiles on other social media sites you and your future clients use. Facebook is a big one. While it's against Facebook's terms and conditions to use a personal profile solely for business purposes, you can absolutely use your personal profile to market and network. Just make sure that's not *all* you do. Be sure your profile isn't stale or impersonal, too. Sometimes attempting to be "professional" just makes you boring. Don't be afraid to inject some real personality into your profile—humans like to work with other humans!

Day 16: Invest in your business.

Do you have the necessary equipment to perform the services you offer? If not, invest in basic equipment to get you started. I suggest quality used equipment when starting, then you can upgrade as you grow. This day can be scary, but you've planned your business and invested in your skill and community. Making sure your equipment is up to par will only make things *easier*, so take a deep breath! It's all good.

By the end of the day today, I want you to have ordered everything you need to get started that you don't already own. One warning: Be careful you don't use your business as an excuse to buy gadgets you don't *need*. This is about investing, not spending. For example, a used or refurbished laptop works just as well as a new one—and it costs less. If you need a kick in the pants here, revisit Chapter 11.

You're as ready as you're going to be *right now*. You already know the "ready" bus will never arrive—because it doesn't exist!

Day 17: Set up a simple website.

A simple, professional website creates a trustworthy online presence. This holds true no matter what kind of client you're seeking. A beautiful, polished website isn't expensive or difficult to set up, either. I still laugh at myself when I think of how long I procrastinated starting Proofread Anywhere just because I didn't know how to create a website!

To help you set up your first budget-friendly, professional website, I put together a ridiculously thorough step-by-step guide you can use. Head over to the Resources page and search for "website tutorial" to quickly find the link... and get started!

Day 18: Practice building relationships.

Using your list of potential clients and influencers from Days 13 and 14—and your updated social media profiles—start interacting. Share, like, or comment on their posts. Add *value* to them. Be generous! Do not spam them or make your initial interaction about getting something from them. The goal here is simply to get on their radar.

If you see someone on your list talking about a problem, comment with some encouragement and/or gratitude for the post, then mention how you've personally experienced something similar and what solution you found. This kind of interaction shows you're not just prowling social media trying to cheaply drum up engagement. Quality commenting showcases your expertise and demonstrates you understand your target client. Bonus... if you comment on a blog post, you can leave a link back to your own website or social profile.

Day 19: Gather references or testimonials.

Have you provided a version of this service for anyone, either paid or for free? If so, let them know that you're building a business around that skill. Ask them if they would be willing to write three sentences recommending you. If they're busy, write the testimonial for them and send it to them saying you're looking for something similar. Many times, they'll reply and let you use it as is.

Here's a template you or your clients can use for writing testimonials:

Before I met [YOUR NAME], I was frustrated with
_____ , but then I met [YOUR NAME]
and he/she _____ so I could finally
_____! I would absolutely recommend
[YOUR NAME] if you want to _____
better in your business.

Be creative. If you're connected with your client or friend on LinkedIn, ask them to leave it there and then copy and paste it onto your website. Grab a screenshot any time you can; people sometimes dismiss written testimonials as embellished or fake.

Video interviews are also a *strong* form of social proof that is hard to argue with! You can use free video conferencing software like Zoom to record an short interview with your client or friend, then just upload it to YouTube and add it to a page on your website. I did exactly this when I started Proofread Anywhere. I interviewed the last person I trained for free and worked that video into my website as a testimonial. Even though that person hadn't taken my course, she was still trained by me. The video was so effective that I still use it today!

Day 20: Get business cards.

Time to order business cards! I recommend carrying at least 25 business cards at all times so you can hand them out whenever an opportunity arises. You never know when that'll be, either—I've handed out business cards at a Super Bowl party! Everyone in your circle should know what you do. That doesn't mean you beat your Aunt Sally over the head with sales pitches every time you see her, but you get my point. Don't be shy!

Get simple, inexpensive business cards at Moo.com or VistaPrint.com. You can even design your own for free using high-quality templates on Canva.com.

Day 21: Practice writing a proposal.

No matter what skill you're selling, potential clients may ask you for a proposal. Now that you know what you're selling, to whom, and for how much, take today to practice writing a proposal.

Open up a fresh Google Doc or Word file. First, describe the skills you're selling. Second, identify how your services help your ideal client. Third, suggest how your clients can measure the results of your services. Fourth, detail what their investment will be for your services.

Once you have a draft, keep it in a safe place. You'll be ready to personalize it for your first (or next) paying client with a few tweaks!

Day 22: Find local networking opportunities.

In most cases, local, in-person networking is the fastest way to get a business off the ground. That's because people can get to know you, shake your hand, and look you in the eyes. In person, you make a much deeper and faster connection than you do online. When you're first starting out, get out from behind your desk and meet people. It's a great way to boost confidence!

Today, identify at least three networking opportunities you can attend within the next 30 days and schedule them on your calendar. Look for Small Business Association meetings, networking meetings, or informal get-togethers. Meetup.com is a great place to look for local networking opportunities, so sign up for free account and start searching.

Also look for at least one opportunity to network locally with your *peers*. Other people in your niche aren't competitors; they're potential teammates. Over time, you could build a strong business referral network among yourselves.

Day 23: Go to your networking meetups and contact five people from your prospect list.

With one exception, you'll spend the rest of the launch plan doing two things. First, you'll continue to develop your skills. Second, you'll interact with people. Contact prospects and influencers. Schedule meetings. Build relationships—and do any work people send your way!

In the upcoming days of the plan, I'll walk you through some ideas and suggestions to keep you moving forward. Your activities may change as your schedule fills with appointments or client work. The important thing is to consistently reach out. Relationships don't build themselves!

Start by reaching out to at least five prospects today. Keep it low pressure. Avoid being salesy or pitching people—this is about networking and letting people know what you're doing. If they invite you out to coffee or lunch, travel to their neighborhood. Make it *easy* for them.

When you're with a prospect, focus on how you might be able to help *them*—not how they can help you. Ask about them and their business. Ask how they got started. Ask what they like best and worst about their business, and listen carefully when they tell you both. Especially when business owners tell you what annoys them about their business, you get *major* clues as to problems you could potentially solve for them. That's the magic of asking!

Think about people you might be able to introduce them to who could potentially help them grow their business. The more helpful you can be to them, the better. At the end, make sure you pick up the check. Don't pitch anything outright unless the prospect makes it clear they're interested in what you offer.

A day or two later, follow up with an email (or better, a handwritten note!) thanking the prospect for their time. Refer them to a resource or colleague to help with a problem, or offer them a service. The fortune is in the follow-up, so don't skip this step! If you don't get a response, don't worry—make a note in your calendar to circle back in two or three months to check in with them.

The goal for these meetings is to build real relationships with people. The best way to do that is to be helpful. To quote the late and great Zig Ziglar one more time, "If you go out looking for friends, you're going to find they are very scarce. If you go out to be a friend, you'll find them everywhere." The same thing is true in business. If you go out looking for support, you'll find it scarce. If you go out looking to be supportive, you'll find support everywhere.

Day 24: Develop your skills and reach out to five more people.

If you have an appointment or networking opportunity scheduled today, go. Then call or email five more people. If you don't have an appointment scheduled, contact five more people.

When someone asks how they can help you, talk about the simple, irresistible offers you have. If you want to write blog posts, you might say, "I'd be happy to write a blog post for your site to show you what I can do. I typically charge $250 per post (or whatever you charge), but I'm trying to collect LinkedIn recommendations to attract more clients. I'd love to write a post for you in exchange for an honest review I can use on LinkedIn and my website."

Day 25: Keep it up.

This is a numbers game. The more people you contact, the faster you can secure paying gigs. Invest 30 minutes today developing either the skills you sell or your business skills. Invest any extra time you have on building relationships.

Reach out to people by phone, text, email, or even social media. Keep commenting, liking, and sharing their posts. Make it a point to invest at least 30 minutes per week doing this until you reach "capacity"—that's when you have enough work! If you run out of prospects or influencers on your list, then work on adding 10 new prospects to your list.

Keep your prospect and *their* problems as #1 at all times. Anytime you meet or chat with a prospect, ask them what connections *you* can make for *them*. If they tell you and no one immediately comes to mind, that's okay. Make a note of the types of people they want to meet, then find someone who can help. Do the research for them! It's a simple service that saves so much time. Going out of your way to solve their problem sans expectation makes an *excellent* impression (speaking from experience)! The more helpful you can be to a prospect, the more likely they'll be to remember—or recommend!—you in the future.

Day 26: Become the grass.

Can I confess something? My only goal with the rest of the launch plan is to get you to make what you've been doing since Day 1 a *habit*. Look back on the last 25 days. What's been working so far? Do more of that.

I want you to get into the habit of taking at least 30 minutes per day to work on developing your skills. Make it a goal to get 1% better every day. Even that small of a percentage, over time, leads to *massive* change. Think about how you never see grass growing, yet after a month of summer sun, that "slow" grass can completely take over your yard. *Become the grass.* It's slow but mighty.

As you build your skills, keep investing time in building relationships. So reach out to at least five more people today. If you're an introvert like me, this can be an anxiety-inducing task, but I assure you that with practice it gets much easier. At least it *feels* that way—the reality is that it *doesn't* get easier; you just get better.

Keep in mind that the more you refine your skills, the more confident you'll feel marketing yourself. If you've found yourself skipping the skills development part and your confidence is shaky at best, *slow down.* Many of my proofreading students begin their course believing that all they *really* need to learn is how to market themselves. Once they get into the meat of the training, they're often shocked at what they don't know. It's a slice of humble pie.

Day 27: Press on... and share your journey.

Continue reinforcing your new business-building habits. Just like yesterday, invest 30 minutes developing your skills and the rest of your available time reaching out to key people and building relationships.

On Day 8 you sought out a community you could turn to for support—and where you could provide support as well. Head over to that community now and post an update on what actions you've taken so far, results you've achieved, feedback you've received, and any questions you may have. If you're in the Work-At-Home Heroes community on Facebook, use the hashtag #share. Once you've posted, you can click that live hashtag to see similar posts from your peers to see feedback they've gotten from the community. If you have something constructive to add to the conversation, chime in!

Day 28: Keep it up... and settle in.

If there were a secret ingredient to the Skills x Action equation for success, *consistency is it.* In fact, just add that word in front of "action" in the equation if you like. If the number you plug in for "Action" is ever a zero, that's not good. Even small actions every day will result in more success than taking no action at all. So settle in. Keep reaching out to your prospects and adding new ones to your list. Continue investing at least 30 minutes per day developing your skills. All these small actions you take—*if* you take them consistently—will pay off. The only way you can fail is if you give up.

Here are some questions you can ask yourself to decide your next steps. What types of people have you built the best relationships with so far? Do you need to meet more prospects? Do you need to meet more peers to share resources and build a referral network? Start reaching out to people in categories where you don't have many contacts.

Take a few minutes today to assess your progress, too. What's going well? What's not going very well? What skills do you need or want to develop? Write down your answers to these questions so you can keep making progress. Feel free to share your answers to these questions in your support community for feedback from your peers.

Many, *many* people give up by this time because they feel like things should be happening faster. If they aren't millionaires overnight, they give up, declare the whole thing a scam, and go back to their old lives feeling defeated and depressed. Here's the reality: *28 days is not a lot of time*. Remember the quote from Bill Gates I shared in Chapter 8? He said, "Most people overestimate what they can do in one year and underestimate what they can do in ten years." The people who quit after just 28 days have grossly overestimated what's realistic in an even shorter amount of time. They don't even give themselves the courtesy of a full year. Don't be one of those people. Building a business takes time. The time will pass anyway, remember... so you might as well invest it into building a life you love instead of living a life you don't!

FINAL WORDS
OF WISDOM

You did it! You got a detailed look at how my completely average life became a success story without any magic or scams—but with plenty of mistakes. You saw how I escaped minimum wage. Then you uncovered and freed your mind of the lies that hold you back. You identified the right work-from-anywhere opportunity for you and started investing in building your skills. You learned how to spot and avoid scams and, hopefully, you completed the 28-day launch plan.

You already have everything you need to create the income and the freedom you want and deserve. It's between your ears. It's your *mind*. Get your mindset right by throwing out all the lies you grew up believing about money, work, education, and success. Replace that crap with new, empowering beliefs. Fill your brain with information and skills, then *take action*. Rinse, lather, repeat. Refuse to give up. This is *your* income story.

Many of my students tell me I seem to read their minds and even haunt them with my no-nonsense messages. It's unrealistic to expect you to reread this entire book every time you need a swift kick in the pants to keep making progress on your journey, so I've created a solution for that. I've gathered the most important concepts from the book in this final chapter so you can easily look back and remind yourself of any of them whenever you need to. I call them golden nuggets.

Replacing garbage with gold is a lifelong process. Occasionally, some lies you used to believe will resurface. The more truth you can "marinate" in during the day, the more power you take away from the lies. *It's all a choice.* In your choices, you have power.

You can start with the skills you have. It might not make you a ton of money at first, but that's no reason to worry—because increasing your income is simple. Just improve or add to your skills. Mo' skills = mo' money, remember? Don't forget it.

To make this real, you have to *want* it. Some people say they want a better life for themselves and their family, but they aren't willing to do anything differently to get it. You've got to *do something* if you want this life—this freedom—for yourself. Refuse to let *anything* stand in the way... especially not yourself.

You have the power to change your whole world—you just need to decide. *Decide* to free your mind of lies. *Decide* to learn powerful skills. *Decide* to take action consistently. *Decide* not to give up. It's all a choice. Your choices can be either your greatest source of power or your biggest weakness. Choose power. Choose *you*.

There is life beyond that stupid thing you did 5, 10, 20, or 30+ years ago. It's safe to move forward. *Now.* You don't need anyone's permission to do it, either.

Fear *never* goes away; it just changes its outfit... and *we* get better at taking action no matter how scary the outfit gets. Look at fear as a tool to gauge your potential for growth. If the thing you want to do isn't scary at all, then you're not going to grow from it. If it's easy, then you won't learn anything new. Good things happen when you act in spite of fear. Facing fear always makes us stronger.

The difference between people who succeed and people who fail is simple. Successful people just never give up. People who fail often never really failed; they just gave up. They stopped trying, while the successful people refused defeat.

> *"Our truest life is when we are in dreams awake."*
> HENRY DAVID THOREAU

> *"There is only one success: to be able to*
> *spend your life in your own way."*
> CHRISTOPHER MORLEY

There is life-changing power when you choose to believe the *truth* instead of lies. And it *is* a choice.

The moment we can look at ourselves in the mirror and tell ourselves the truth about how we've been living, we give ourselves the power we need to transform. So commit to telling yourself the truth and doing whatever it takes to train your brain to *believe* that truth. You deserve to live your life that way!

Real power comes not from knowing stuff; it comes from *doing* stuff with what you know. There's power in the sheer admission that you don't know everything—and that if you learn something new, you can *do* something new. If you do something new, then you'll get something new… which could be mo' money than you ever thought you'd see in your lifetime!

Start. Then do *not* give up, even if it's been more than six months; even if it's been more than a year. Because the thing is, the time will pass anyway… it might even stop for us all together without notice. We can't know exactly when our time is up, so we might as well invest our time wisely and *do the thing. Try* to create the life of your dreams… and see what happens. Let's not get to the end of our lives and wonder where the time went—where *life* went—and why we didn't make better use of it when we had the chance.

Even when it's hard… even when you don't feel like it… even when someone hiding behind a computer screen calls you names, *don't give up.* Keep pushing through when you think you've failed. Master your skill and market it. Be relentless in your pursuit of the life you've dreamed of. You can make it real.

If you sit and wait for all the ducks in your life to line up on their own before you go anywhere, you'll be waiting—*doing nothing*—for a long time. That's not what you want, is it? So the best solution is to effect your own change. Take action. Pick up one of those ducks and *run* with it. See what happens. More often than not, the rest of the ducks will follow!

Even taking a step onto an ugly stepping stone is far better than not taking a step at all. A step is a step, and every step is an opportunity to learn something new. The job you may feel is "beneath" you can actually elevate you.

Your ability to make money is a result of 1) the choices you make and 2) the actions you take.

Don't get caught up in the endless vortex of research trying to see the entire staircase before you take the first step. For many of us, the staircase isn't even there yet because you'll be building it yourself—one step at a time.

The "ready bus" doesn't exist. Quit waiting for it. You wouldn't be reading this right now if you weren't already ready *enough* to get started.

You don't get traction without action. It's a law of physics. Waiting will do nothing. Waiting *is* doing nothing—and you're meant to do far more than nothing.

You can.

To your success,

Caitlin

P.S. — Grab a printable PDF of these quotes at WorkAtHomeSchool. com/BookResources along with your free lifetime access to the Work-At-Home Summit.

ACKNOWLEDGMENTS

L et's start from the very beginning...

To my parents, Lyle Roll and Maria Nifong... obviously, without you both, I wouldn't be here. Literally. I love you (also literally).

To my sister, Courtney... thank you for your support—and for your forgiveness for all the times I wasn't my best self.

To all the kids who were mean to me in middle school... we'll keep your resume on file for six months. You'll hear from us if we're interested.

To my husband, Ben... without your gentle-yet-consistent nudges, I never would've believed I could even start a website. Thank you for being my rock—and for allowing me to roll. I will always admire your patience, understanding, and ability to withstand the gale-force winds of Hurricane Me. Can you believe we're here?! Can you imagine where we're going... and how many incredible people are coming along?!

To my other parents, Ken and Sheila Pyle, and to Stephanie Pyle (my bonus sister!)... thank you for being three of my biggest fans throughout this crazy journey! Your support means more to me than I could ever express. I love you so much.

To the winning personalities who fired me in August 2011 and said I'd die alone... you gave me the exact "failure" I needed to succeed.

To the past and present members of my team who made both me and this book possible... Katie Chase, Elizabeth Wiegner, Jonathan Wiegner, Tara Whitaker, Maia Xiong, Maria Arellano, April Thompson, Brittany Long, Julie Stoian, David Gonzalez, Gonzalo Paternoster, Tonya Williams, Nick Pavlidis, Jennifer Harshman, Talia Browne, Steve Stewart, Joe Schmitz, Daniel Reifenberger, Tina Lorenz, Billy Broas... thank you all for your loyalty and support.

To my remarkable clients who put their faith in my abilities to grow their businesses like a weed: Janet Shaughnessy and Linda Evenson, thank you for challenging me in the best of ways to not just grow your businesses, but to grow myself in the process. I am your #1 fan.

To 48+ partners who aligned with me to share the message of Work-At-Home School with the world... thank you for your generosity. You think BIG; you think LEGACY. I am so honored to be your teammate.

To Mary and Barry Blanton, Jenna and Aaron Bachman, Lee Cason, Molly MacCartney, Robbie and Melissa Stephenson, Tina and Gene Propper, Noah Nifong, Michael Eckert, and Taylor Brown: thank you for being my friends and for always cheering me on.

To my personal assistant, Paris McElroy, thank you for never judging me for the messes I make—or the ones I get myself into!

Lastly, thank you to my publisher, Morgan James—without you guys, the words in this book would still be floating around in my head. Thank you for helping me get this message into the hands of the people who need it.

ABOUT THE AUTHOR
Caitlin Pyle

Caitlin Pyle graduated summa cum laude from the University of Central Florida in 2009, but she'll be the first to tell you that was *not* the path to the freedom she now enjoys. Although she's now a self-made millionaire entrepreneur, she had to get out of her own way first. Now she gives no-nonsense, "swift kick in the butt" advice on how *you* can get out of your own way, build skills, and create income—so you can live the life of your dreams, too.

After getting fired in 2011, Caitlin built her skills into a $40k+/year income with a thriving freelance proofreading business. In 2014, she started her first blog; and in 2015 launched her first online course, *Transcript Proofreading: Theory and Practice*™, which generated $100k+ in just three months.

And that was just the beginning. Caitlin launched another course in 2017, *General Proofreading: Theory and Practice*™, this time with over a million dollars made in eight months alone!

In 2018, Caitlin launched the revolutionary online Work-At-Home School, *the* one-stop place to build your work-at-home life from the ground up.

Caitlin, her husband Ben, and their über-cute Swedish Vallhund, Buffett, live in Winter Park, Florida in their dream home Caitlin designed herself using just graph paper and a pencil... all while living in Argentina!

 Morgan James makes all of our titles available
through the Library for All Charity Organization.

www.LibraryForAll.org